THE PANTHER TANK

DR MATTHEW HUGHES
&
DR CHRIS MANN

THE PANTHER TANK

DR MATTHEW HUGHES & DR CHRIS MANN

SPELLMOUNT
Staplehurst

British Library Cataloguing in Publication Data:
A catalogue record for this book is available
from the British Library

ISBN 1-86227-072-4

First published in the UK in 2000 by
Spellmount Limited
The Old Rectory
Staplehurst
Kent TN12 0AZ

1 3 5 7 9 8 6 4 2

Editorial and design: Amber Books Ltd
Bradley's Close, 74-77 White Lion Street,
London N1 9PF

Editor: Vanessa Unwin
Design: Hawes Design

Printed and bound in The Slovak Republic
60316

Picture credits
The Robert Hunt Library: 26, 28, 30, 33, 38, 43, 47,
48-49, 52, 58, 65, 66-67, 69, 74, 81(t), 84, 86-87, 89, 90.
Salamander Books: 22-23, 61, 72-73. TRH Pictures: 6-7
(Tank Museum Collection), 8, 9, 11, 12, 13, 14-15 (Tank
Museum Collection), 18, 24, 27, 29 (US National Archives) 31
(US National Archives), 32, 36, 37 (US National Archives), 42
(US National Archives), 52-53, 54, 59, 60-61, 63, 64, 70 (US
National Archives), 71, 74-75, 76-77 (US National Archives),
77 (US National Archives), 80 (US Air Force), 81(b)
(US National Archives), 82, 83 (US National Archives).
Martin Windrow: 16-17, 19, 40-41, 50, 55, 68.

Artwork credits
Aerospace Publishing: 34-35, 44-45, 62, 78-79, 88, 91.
John Bachelor: 56-57. Ray Hutchins: 20-21. Orbis Publishing:
51.

Front cover
Artwork: Aerospace Publishing. Bottom left: TRH (Tank
Museum Collection). Bottom right: Robert Hunt Library.

Back cover
Richard Stickland

Pages 2-3: A Panther gives support to panzergrenadiers preparing to meet the Allied invasion forces somewhere in northern France.

CONTENTS

CHAPTER 1

The Origins of the Panther

The Panzerkampfwagen (PzKpfw) V 'Panther' tank was a superb weapon system and was certainly the best German tank design of World War II. Considerably superior to the Shermans, Churchills and Cromwells of the Western Allies, it just about had the edge on its rival for the best tank of the war, the Soviet T-34/85.

Provided the Panther was mechanically sound, had enough fuel to allow the crew to manoeuvre with some freedom (not necessarily a totally safe option, given Allied control of the skies), and adequate ammunition (the supply of tungsten carbide-cored armour piercing rounds ran out in the last months of the war), as well as a reasonably trained crew, the excellent 7.5cm KwK 42 gun and optical sights, thick frontal armour, and the fact the crew were almost certainly fighting a defensive action, made its user the most likely victor in a tank-to-tank engagement against almost any Allied opponent. Whether that victor would defeat the fourth or fifth enemy tank it would almost certainly face in that battle is another matter.

The Panther was designed to wrest the dominance of the battlefields of the Eastern Front from the Soviet T-34. The intention was to produce a tank of such qualitative superiority that it could outfight the T-34 and halt the gathering Soviet offensive momentum. The Panther arguably achieved the former but the latter goal was beyond it. In World War II, quantity mattered the most, particularly in the colossal struggles in the East and, despite the Panther's excellence, the qualitative difference between it and the T-34/85 remained slight. Superb tank that it was, the Panther was complicated, hurriedly rushed into production, and therefore initially plagued by mechanical problems. Difficult to manufacture, it was never available in adequate numbers. It could provide tactical supremacy but, unlike the T-34, the German tank was not a war winner.

Left: The reason for building the Panther: Soviet T-34 medium tanks advancing into battle on the Eastern Front. The T-34 forced the Germans to replace the generation of panzers then in service.

Although the Panther may have been the pinnacle of World War II tank design, for a nation so often at the cutting edge of military technology, Germany was unusually slow in appreciating the revolutionary nature of the tracked armoured fighting vehicle. During World War I the Germans had never seriously considered the possibility of mechanised armoured warfare until the appearance of British tanks at the Battle of the Somme in 1916. Initially, the Germans believed that the tanks, which had been so far used in insufficient numbers on unsuitable ground, had little practical value. However, the continued and increasingly successful use of tanks on the Western Front by the British, and subsequently the French, belatedly convinced the German High Command that their own tanks were required as a countermeasure to the new weapon.

THE FIRST GERMAN TANKS

The German response, the A7V *Sturmpanzerwagon*, was original in both its layout and engineering concept. It was not, however, a particularly good tank. The designers had attempted to achieve engineering ideals beyond Germany's

production capacity and technological expertise. The result – essentially a large armoured box, crewed by 18 men, built on to a modified Holt tractor chassis – was disappointing. Clumsy, underpowered, slow and vulnerable, it was no match for the contemporary British tanks. Furthermore, the A7V was put into production at a time when German industry was terribly overstretched by manufacturing U-boats, artillery and more traditional weapons. Only 20 A7Vs were built and a mere 15 saw combat. Like its distant successor, the Panther, there were nowhere near enough of them. The German Army was forced to rely on British tanks; only three German tank sections were equipped with the A7V, as compared to six which used captured British vehicles.

The Germans also produced a number of improved designs, none of which progressed past the prototype stage before the war ended in November 1918. However, much of the German design and production potential was dissipated on a large number of projects, some of which, to say the very least, stretched the limits of practicality. Particularly notable amongst these was the 150-tonne (148-ton) K-Wagen (*Grosskampfwagen*). This monster, with a crew of 22 men and untransportable on the railway systems of the time, had considerable and obvious difficulties with mobility and movement which allow comparison with some of the more fanciful German tank designs of a quarter century later. To quote the British Royal Armoured Corps Tank Museum, these problems were 'overlooked or discounted in the same way these difficulties were ignored over the Maus and E100 in the Second World War'.

HEINZ GUDERIAN AND CLANDESTINE TANK RESEARCH

The victorious Allied powers imposed considerable limits on Germany's military strength as part of the World War I peace settlement signed at Versailles in June 1919. The Treaty of Versailles forbade Germany the possession of key weapons such as military aircraft, U-boats and heavy artillery. It limited the Reichswehr, as the new restricted German armed forces were called, to 100,000 men. The possession, development, or purchase of tanks – and most other armoured vehicles – was forbidden. The German Army was left with only a few ageing armoured cars and tenders.

The small size of the 100,000 German Army, although it limited promotion opportunities, allowed concentration on quality in both training and methods. The Chief of the German General Staff, General Hans von Seekt, was determined to ensure that the Reichswehr provided as potent and powerful a military force as possible, given its much reduced size. During his tenure, therefore, he gave considerable support to the ideas of Germany's leading tank enthusiast, Heinz Guderian. In 1922, Guderian, during an unwanted posting to

Left: A German tank crew with their short-barrelled Panzer IV, a tank which lacked adequate firepower to deal with the new Soviet tanks such as the KV and T-34. Note the two 'kill rings' on the barrel.

the Inspectorate of Transport Troops, had begun to study the work of the British armoured warfare theorists, J.F.C. Fuller, Basil Liddell Hart and G. LeQ Martel. Fuller and Liddell Hart, who proposed that the wars of the future would be fought by highly mechanised forces based around the tank, were particularly influential. They advocated the concentration of striking forces (the *Schwerpunkt* in German) at the enemy's weak point which would produce a breakthrough. This breakthrough would be exploited by the rapid concentration of all forces into what was known as an 'expanding torrent', which would penetrate deeply into the enemy's rear and disrupt communication and supply routes. Essentially the mechanised troops struck at the enemy's control and logistics mechanisms – the enemy's brain – rather than the opposing front line troops.

According to Guderian, he was 'deeply impressed by these ideas'. He wrote, 'I tried to develop them in a sense practicable for our own army.' Like most of the advocates of armoured warfare in the 1920s, Guderian met with some resistance from within the army. In 1924, when he expressed his wish of transforming the motorised units of the supply troops into combat formations, Guderian was told by his commander, 'To hell with combat, they are supposed to carry flour.' Nonetheless, his superiors were largely supportive and a core of German staff officers began to take seriously the possibility of conducting mobile war based around armoured units. A limited programme of training and close cooperation began in about 1925. In the following year, the first full-scale manoeuvres involving mechanised forces took place. However, Guderian's theorising and ambitious proposals for the formation of armoured units were somewhat

hampered by a complete lack of armoured fighting vehicles because the Treaty of Versailles still banned their possession by the Reichswehr. During the 1926 manoeuvres, in place of tanks, soldiers had to carry cardboard tank silhouettes. By 1928, they had progressed to using 'motorised dummies of sheet metal'. As Guderian himself said, despite his preoccupation, he was 'totally lacking in all practical experience of tanks ... I had never even seen the inside of one'.

This lack of vehicles did not mean that Germany had wholly abandoned research into tank design and production. German engineers had been carrying out clandestine research from 1920 onwards, despite the limitations imposed by the Treaty of Versailles. In the early 1920s, a small cadre had worked in Sweden on the production of the LK II tank. This was a wartime German design, weighing 10.16 tonnes (10 tons), powered by a 50hp. engine to speeds of 19.3km (12mph) and mounting a 37mm gun in a non-revolving turret. The Germans had completed the prototype during World War I and, immediately after the conflict, sold the prototype and the design to Sweden, which built it as the Strv M21/29. Guderian finally managed to inspect the inside of a tank when he visited Sweden in 1928 and even had the opportunity to drive the LK II. The General Staff were determined that Germany should have some tanks of its own and issued a secret specification to German industry to produce prototypes of two types of tank. The first specification was for a light tank mounting a 3.7cm gun. The second was for a

RUSSIAN TANK DEVELOPMENT

Tanks came late to Russia, appearing in the post-Revolution civil wars between the Whites and the communist Reds. The first Soviet tanks were copies of Renault FT tanks, and were designated M-17. An upgraded T-18 was produced in 1925, but the Soviet army remained heavily reliant on cavalry.

However the Russians were keen to develop their armoured forces, and found an unlikely bedmate in Germany. Collaboration between the two countries continued until Hitler ordered it to cease in 1934, by which time both sides had exchanged a considerable amount of knowledge.

Russian tactical and strategic thinking in the late 1920s and 1930s demanded a mechanised, modern army. The Red Army General Staff passed a special directive in 1929 giving priority to tank production, and by 1932 the Red Army had two mechanised corps consisting of armour, motorised infantry, artillery and reconnaissance units, three years before the first Panzer division was formed. Tank production had soared: in 1928 the Soviets had 92 tanks; by January 1935 they had 10,180.

The T-14, the first home-grown medium tank, failed due to problems with its suspension, automotive parts and inadequate armour, although it was armed with a 76mm (3in) gun, a massive weapon for the period. To save time the Soviets bought designs from Carden-Lloyd and Vickers, and from the former they developed the T-27 tankette. The T-26 light tank, derived from a Vickers design upgunned to 45mm (1.77in), was used in the Spanish Civil War, and an improved version was still in service in 1941. The T-28 infantry tank was also still extant, but it too failed to cope with the German panzers.

It was the American Christie M1931 design that gave the Russians their first success. Produced as the BT tank and steadily upgunned, the Soviets had probably the best tank of the mid-1930s, despite its relatively poor showing in the Spanish Civil War.

Unfortunately, the army purges from 1937 onwards severely disrupted the Soviet armoured forces, and loss of so many trained men affected the defence of Russia in 1941. By then, however, the Russians had a number of new tanks: the KV heavy tank, the expensive and complex T-50 light tank, the amphibious T-40, and the T-34. Of all of these, the 76mm (3in) armed T-34 was to prove one of the most successful tanks of World War II, and the direct catalyst for the developement of the Panther.

medium tank of about 20.32 tonnes (20 tons) armed with a 7.5cm gun. This was extremely well armed for its time and shows the German belief, even from a very early stage, that the principal aspect of a tank is its firepower.

The first problem was to find a place to build and test these designs away from the prying eyes of the West. The Germans, eager to circumvent the restraints of the Treaty of Versailles, had turned to their fellow pariah nation, the Soviet Union, which had been shunned by the international community for its Bolshevism. In 1921, the Reichswehr tentatively established its first contacts with its unlikely collaborator, the Red Army. The following year, the two nations signed the Rappallo Treaty which included a secret clause cementing military cooperation. The collaboration was expanded in March 1926 when the Germans established an airfield at Liptesk and a tank school at Kazan on the Volga. It was at Kazan that Germany's first postwar tanks were built. Two German engineering firms, Krupp and Rheinmetall, built three prototypes, each to the light tank specification, known as *Leichter Traktor* (light tractor) to disguise its true nature. This 10.16 tonne (10 ton) vehicle owed much to British designs of the time, resembling a Vickers Medium Mark II. The larger tank, known as the *Grosstraktor*, resembled the Vickers 16-tonner. Daimler-Benz, Krupp and Rheinmetall all produced a prototype of this 17.27 tonne (17-ton) vehicle which was armed with either a 7.5cm (2.95in) gun or a 10.5cm (4.1in) howitzer. These were thoroughly tested at Kazan, although they were not put into production.

Following these trials, a further design was proposed, known as the *Neubaufahrzeug* (new construction vehicle), usually referred to by the acronym NbFz. This was intended to enter service in the mid-1930s, as it was clear from the Kazan trials that the production of modern tanks involved a great deal of industrial and development potential, and would be subject to long delays between conception and full-scale production. Rheinmetall won the contract to design the hull of the NbFz, while Krupp and Rheinmetall produced two different turrets. The designs finally appeared in 1933. The Krupp turret fitted to the NbFz A mounted a 7.5cm gun and a 3.7cm gun coaxially. The Rheinmetall fitted to the NbFz B also had a coaxial arrangement of its 10.5cm and 3.7cm main armament. Both versions also mounted two machine-gun turrets on the hull. This multi-turreted type of design had been used on the British independent tank of 1926 and the Russian T-32 of 1929. However, the multiple turret concept was largely regarded as obsolete by 1933. The numerous turrets produced shot-traps, their crewmen introduced extra weight, and the concept was seen as a blind alley, therefore the Germans never put them into service. Five were built and used purely for training purposes, although some turned up during the German invasion of Norway in 1944. However, these appear only to have been used for propaganda purposes. The NbFz A was given the designation PzKpfw V, and the NbFz B given the designation

PzKpfw VI. This can cause some confusion because the designations PzKpfw V and PzKpfw VI were later given to the more famous Panther and Tiger tanks respectively. During the crisis of the national economy of 1930, when all money was withdrawn from the tank programme, German tank experiments came to a fairly abrupt end.

Guderian – who by 1932 was a lieutenant colonel, and chief of staff to the inspectorate of motorised troops – and Captain Pirner, responsible for tank production, worked out the eventual equipment of the Panzer divisions Guderian was so keen to establish. They agreed that they needed two types of tank: a light tank equipped with an armoured piercing gun in the turret; and a medium tank with a larger calibre weapon. They settled on a 3.7cm (1.45in) gun for the light tank and a 7.5cm (2.95in) for the medium which was not to exceed 24.38 tonnes (24 tons) in weight. The limiting factor was the capacity of the German road bridges. These were long-range plans, as it was clear that it would take a long time for these tanks to enter service. In the meantime, a stop gap was needed, something that was easy to build and could be built in large numbers. The other criteria were that it could be used for training and could give the proposed armoured units experience of mechanised warfare.

HITLER AND THE EARLY PANZERS

In 1933, Adolf Hitler became Chancellor of Germany. Things began to move fast for Guderian and his armoured force. Hitler was less interested in the restrictions imposed by

Versailles and was determined to build up German military strength. In December of that year, Krupp submitted a design for a light training tank, based on the British Carden-Loyd Mark VI tankette which the Germans had thoroughly tested at Kazan. The 5.08 tonne- (5-ton) Krupp design was disguised under the name *Landwirtschafticher Schlepper* (agricultural tractor abbreviated to LaS) and was in production by 1934. It was later given the designation of PzKpfw I. This training tank was scarcely a practical combat vehicle. Crewed by two men, with a maximum of 13mm (0.51in) of armour, a four-cylinder Krupp M105 engine giving a road speed of 40kph (24.85mph), and armed with two machine guns, it could only be used against infantry and soft-skinned vehicles. The PzKpfw I was utterly ineffective against other armoured vehicles. Hitler visited the army ordnance testing ground at Kummersdorf to see Guderian's new tanks in action. When he saw the PzKpfw I, he remarked, 'That's what I need. That's what I want to have.' For the army, the PzKpfw I was perfect for training and experimental manoeuvres; Hitler liked it because it was cheap and he could have lots of them. Although of little combat value, it looked impressive, made an excellent platform for impromptu pieces of Hitler's rhetoric and, because it was so readily available, could be provided in large numbers to intimidate foreign visitors.

Below: A driver's view of battle: a T-34 in action. The T-34's armour gave it almost total protection against all German anti-tank weapons in 1941, due to its thickness and slope.

Above: A Soviet tank factory somewhere in the Urals. Although forced to relocate to the east after the German invasion, Soviet tank production soon outpaced that of the Germans.

The army, however, was well aware that it needed a more practical design to fill the gap before the larger tanks were ready to enter service. The PzKpfw II was a MAN (*Maschinenfabrik Augsburg-Nürnberg*) design. It resembled a scaled-up PzKpfw I, but was heavier and used a revised suspension system. It was a larger vehicle, initially weighing 7.62 tonnes (7.5 tons), although it was up-armoured in 1937 to bring it over 10.16 tonnes (10 tons) and was armed with a 2cm gun. It was a more battle-worthy tank than its predecessor, but not much more. However, these two tanks, produced in large numbers (1500 of the PzKpfw I and 1400 of the PzKpfw II), were the mainstay of the German Panzer armies until 1939.

These light tanks allowed Guderian to develop his theories of armoured warfare. Guderian was unique amongst armoured theorists in the support he received from his superiors and his government. The British, who had developed the most advanced armoured forces in the mid- and late 1920s, had rejected Fuller and Liddell Hart's theories, rele-

gating the tank to an infantry support role and closing down the 'experimental mechanised force'. The Americans and French had not even been allowed to form a separate armoured corps. Admittedly, Marshal Mikhail Tukhachevsky had been able to train and equip large-scale armoured formations in the Soviet Union, but he and his theories were swept away by Stalin's purge of the military from 1937 onwards. Guderian's theories were not particularly different from those put forward by the British and Tukhachevsky. Where he differed from most, however, was that he saw tanks as only truly effective in combination with other arms. Very little of his basic theory was challenged by his superiors. His belief in a rapid war of movement conformed to Prussian military thought since the elder Moltke and was in a direct line of descendance from the German stormtrooper tactics of World War I.

In 1935, the French formed the world's first armoured division. Although there was nothing revolutionary about the French use of tanks, this spurred the Germans to form their own. Thankfully, there were enough PzKpfws available to form three, but this was not a particularly seminal development. What was important was the way in which Guderian welded these Panzer divisions into an effective fighting force. In the Panzer division, Guderian successfully combined sufficient power for the assault on the enemy position with the mobility needed for the pursuit. The Panzer division was an integrated formation carrying its own infantry which were available to clear up any pockets of enemy resistance left behind by the tanks. They could also take the lead if the terrain did not suit armoured operations. The division was supported by its own assault guns which could open avenues of light resistance located by the division's reconnaissance vehicles. It also had its own artillery to deal with the opposition which could not be silenced by the tanks' weaponry. The Germans pioneered the use of dive-bombers as close support in place of an artillery which might clutter up the roads behind the armoured spearhead.

After the re-occupation of the Rhineland in 1936, the Germans began to deploy their tanks openly. The pretence of referring to their tanks as tractors and other innocuous names was dropped. They also had the opportunity to test their theories under battlefield conditions when the Condor Legion was sent to Spain to support Franco's nationalist rebels. Although the Germans probably gained more experience of air warfare in Spain during the Civil War, they also

deployed a number of PzKpfw I tanks. These tanks proved hopelessly out-gunned by Soviet T-26 tanks with 45mm (1.77in) cannons, but it gave the German Army practical experience of operating tanks in combat and taught it some useful lessons in logistics and maintenance, at which it later excelled. Importantly, unlike the Soviets, the German Army did not draw any erroneous lessons from the conflict.

Guderian was promoted to Lieutenant General and given command of the world's first armoured corps over several officers senior to him. He was given command of the spearhead of the German force assigned to undertake the annexation of Austria, known as the Anschluss. This gave him the opportunity to demonstrate the capacity of his tank units, since long distance cross-country movement deployed for possible combat as resistance could not be entirely discounted. For the Germans, the Anschluss was a political success but a military failure. Guderian's corps performed badly and it highlighted all the logistical problems of the Panzer

Below: The PAK-40 75mm (2.95in) anti-tank gun was one of the few available that could knock out a T-34, and the weapon was the basic model for the Panther's main armament, with an increase in calibre.

Above: The first production model of the Panther, the Ausf D. The sleek silhouette and sloping armour betray its debt to the T-34. The Ausf D can be distinguished by the radio-operator's machine gun slot.

divisions. Mechanical failures ran to considerably more than the 30 per cent admitted by the Germans. Tanks ran out of fuel and Guderian was forced to threaten violence in order to use a fuel depot. As a result of his experiences in Austria, Guderian always ensured that his divisions carried between three to five days' supply of fuel, food and ammunition and that his supply services were carefully integrated into the formation.

WAR

German war plans had always been based around conflict breaking out in 1942 at the earliest. By then, the German armed forces, known since the rise of Hitler as the Wehrmacht, would be equipped with a level of arms appropriate for conflict with the West. By the time Hitler invaded Poland on 1 September 1939, the bulk of German armoured forces remained the PzKpfw I and II. Fortunately, the peaceful incorporation of Czechoslovakia into the German Reich had provided the Wehrmacht with large numbers of the Czech Army's excellent LT-35 and LT-38 tanks, built at the Skoda works in Pilsen. These were known, in German service, as the PzKpfw 35 (t) and PzKpfw 38 (t) respectively. The Polish Army lacked modern equipment and had very few tanks and thus was subject to the first application of Guderian's theories which soon became known in the Western press as Blitzkrieg, or Lightning War. Poland fell in 18 days. This was an astounding victory. Admittedly, most of the German army remained foot bound and its artillery was

ous to all German tank weaponry of the time. The Germans essentially had too few well-armed tanks. However, the reason they defeated the British and French in May and June 1940 was due to the high quality of training of their armoured formations, their use of close air support, and the soundness of Guderian's doctrine of Blitzkrieg.

THE INVASION OF THE SOVIET UNION

France had possessed roughly three times the number of tanks belonging to the Germans and their quality was roughly the same. Where the Germans had proved superior was on tactics and training. The fall of France was the high benchmark of Guderian's Blitzkrieg. In June 1941, Hitler turned his attention to the Soviet Union. The Germans had learnt some lessons in France; the PzKpfw III had proved very useful, but it needed more armour and a larger gun. Hitler, who had always taken a personal interest in the Panzer arms, ordered that it be re-equipped with a 5cm (1.96in) L/60 gun. In direct contravention to this, the models F, G and H were armed with a 5cm L/42 calibre weapon. This proved to be a serious tactical error when it came across the best tanks in the Soviet arsenal. The PzKpfw IV had also proved to be very successful in France and the subsequent campaign in Greece. Fighting the British Matilda and the French Char B, the PzKpfw IV was seen to be undergunned. Thus, it was upgunned from a L/43 weapon to a 7.5cm L/48, capable of taking on any Western tank, and also giving it a reasonable chance against the best tanks the Soviets could offer. However, there were very few of these available for Operation Barbarossa, the invasion of the Soviet Union.

In June 1941, when Germany invaded the Soviet Union, the Wehrmacht had 5264 tanks of all types, excluding captured French vehicles. Of these, there were 1440 PzKpfw III and 517 PzKpfw IV frontline tanks. These faced 20,000–24,000 Soviet tanks. Once again, the German Blitzkrieg met with initial success and, for the loss of 2700 vehicles, the Germans destroyed 17,000 Soviet tanks. However, there was no qualitative superiority. Although the PzKpfw III and the PzKpfw IV were considerably better than the Soviet T-26 and BT tanks, nonetheless, they were no match for the latest tank in the Soviet armoured force, the T-34. Mikhail Koskhin's T-34 left a lasting impression on those German Panzer troops who survived meeting it. Its powerful 76.2mm gun could penetrate the armour of all German tanks at almost any combat range and its sloped armour was impervious to the Wehrmacht's standard 3.7cm anti-tank gun, the 5cm gun mounted on the PzKpfw III, and the 7.5cm weapon on the PzKpfw IV. Up until the Soviet campaign, the Germans had had no intention of replacing the PzKpfw IV as it had performed so well in the campaigns in the West. However, the myth of Soviet inferiority had been rudely dispelled, and the Germans desperately needed a new tank which could beat the T-34. This need set in motion the series of events that led to the building of the Panther.

towed by horses, but the armoured formations supported by artillery and the Luftwaffe amply proved that Guderian's theories were right.

The balance of power between Germany and the Western Allies was far closer than between Poland and the Wehrmacht. The Germans were finally beginning to receive the medium tanks ordered in the mid-1930s in some numbers. In the PzKpfw III, the Germans had finally produced a true battle tank. Armed with a 3.7cm gun, the PzKpfw III was a good all-round medium tank. There had only been 98 available for the campaign in Poland. However, these began to make the bulk of German armoured forces by May 1940 in conjunction with the low-velocity armed PzKpfw IV. These were both sound tank designs, but the British and French possessed vehicles which were equal or better, such as the Somua-35, the Char B and the Matilda-II, which was impervi-

CHAPTER 2

Design and Layout of the Panther

The appearance of the T-34 had a profound effect on the invading German troops. The first real sighting was by the 17th German Panzer Division on 8 July 1941. A single, unfamiliar tank appeared on the horizon which proceeded to cut a 14.5km (9-mile) swathe through the advancing division. It was apparently invulnerable to the guns of the Germans' PzKpfw IIIs. Before it was stopped by a 100mm (3.94in) artillery piece which the Germans managed to get behind it, the lone T-34 had destroyed around 40 German armoured vehicles.

When met in larger numbers, the T-34 – and also the KV I heavy tank – could cause the Germans considerable problems, as when massed T-34 tanks gave the 4th Panzer Division a brutal mauling in October 1941. It was a tank absolutely superior to anything belonging to the Germans and the myth of German invincibility was seriously shaken. The T-34's apparent invulnerability had a detrimental effect on the German troops' morale as they felt they had no weapons which could adequately deal with it. To quote Henry Metalman, a Panzer tank driver, 'I pulled up in my tank next to it and I looked at the T-34 and I looked at my, well, what you could call cigarette box in comparison. I thought, well, if I have to confront that tank, I haven't got a chance.'

The concern caused by the appearance of the T-34 went higher up the ranks than just the men who had to face it. It was clear to Guderian that the Germans needed a weapon to counter the new Soviet tank and must hurriedly reconsider their own tank development programme. There had been no plans to replace the PzKpfw IV at the time, after the tank's success in earlier campaigns. Guderian summed up the situation facing him in late 1941:

Left: Testing an Ausf D just off the production line in 1943. The early models of the Panther were plagued with teething problems and most required modifications before being ready for the front.

Above: A view showing the long-barrelled 75mm (2.95in) KwK 42 L/70 main armament, which was effective against almost all the contemporary Allied tanks at long range.

'Numerous T-34s went into action and inflicted heavy losses on the German tanks. Up to this time, we had enjoyed tank superiority, but from now on the situation was reversed. The prospect of rapid, decisive victories was fading in consequence. I made a report on this situation, which for us was a new one, and sent it to the Army Group; in this report I described in plain terms the marked superiority of the T-34 to our Panzer IV and drew the relevant conclusions as they must affect our future tank production. I concluded by urging that a commission be sent immediately to my sector of the front and that it consist of representatives of the Army Ordnance Office, the armaments Ministry, the tank designers and the firms which build the tanks ... The officers at the front were of the opinion that the T-34 should simply be copied, since this would be the quickest way of putting to rights the most unhappy situation of the German Panzer troops.'

THE PZKPFW III AND IV REPLACEMENT PROGRAMME

The origins of the Panther's design can be traced back to 1938 when the *Waffenprüfamt Sechs* (Wa Prüf 6), the section of the army's weapons department (*Heereswaffenamt*) responsible for armoured fighting vehicle design and procurement, issued a specification for a replacement of the PzKpfw III and IV. Ernest Kniepkamp of Wa Prüf 6 provided specific instructions as to what he wanted on the chassis of the new tank design: large road wheels; torsion bar suspension; the latest motor design; power assisted semi-automatic

transmissions; and advanced steering gear designs. The German system of weapon procurement is worthy of a short note. The Wa Prüf 6 was responsible for providing a vehicle specification and then sponsoring competitive designs from different private firms. It would accept the model it considered best and modify as it saw necessary. This system had manifested itself as early as the armoured car designs of 1915 and lasted until the end of World War II. It was reasonably flexible; often firms would be ordered to cooperate in times of need, and production orders might be spread across numerous manufacturers, even to failed competitors if high levels of output were required.

The first contract for a vehicle in the 20.32-tonne (20-ton) class was issued to Daimler-Benz and designated VK 2001. The VK 2001 was a completely new design and was one of the first tanks with a *Schactellaufwerk* (interleaved road wheel suspension) system. The advantage of this system was a shorter ground contact length, which improved steering, distributing the tank's weight over larger diameter road wheels. Larger diameter road wheels lasted longer and provided a smoother ride over rough terrain. They also lowered bogie drag and increased the running life of the tyres. Most previous German tank designs had small diameter bogies. This interleaved arrangement was used in the final design of the Panther. Daimler-Benz decided to equip the VK 2001 with an MB 809 diesel motor which was ready by June 1940.

Kniepkamp had also approached Krupp to design a version of the VK 2001. In May 1940, Krupp produced a design

Right: A turret being fitted in a German factory. Panthers were produced in four main factories: MAN (Nürnberg), Daimler-Benz (Berlin), Henschel und Sohn (Kassel) and MNH (Hannover).

PzKpfw V Panther Ausf G

1 75mm (2.95in) L/70 gun
2 7.92mm (0.31in) MG34 machine gun
3 7.92mm (0.31in) MG34 machine gun
4 Ventilator
5 Commander's cupola
6 Gun cradle
7 Sighting telescope TZF 12a
8 Loading/escape hatch
9 Commander's headset
10 Wireless operator's hatch
11 Turret traversing gear
12 Elevation handwheel

38 Final drive
39 Sprocket
40 Return roller
41 Limited suspension stop
42 Shock absorber
43 Swing-arm bearing bracket
44 Suspension crank arm
45 Interleaved road wheels
46 Idler wheel
47 Torsion-bar suspension

13 Engine ventilator
14 Cooling air inlet
15 75mm (2.95in) ammunition
16 Balance/elevating   gear
17 Gun compensator/balance
18 Spent 75mm (2.95in)
    cartridge bin
19 Maybach engine
20 Gun cleaning kit
21 Spare track links
22 7.92mm (0.31in)
    MG34 machine gun
    ammunition
23 Gunner's seat
24 Wireless
    operator's seat
25 Instrument panel
26 Spent 7.92mm
    (0.31in) MG34
    machine gun
    ammunition container
27 Hydraulic traversing unit
28 Compressor
29 Brake link
30 Steering lever
31 Driver's seat
32 7.92mm (0.31in) MG34 machine gun firing pedal
33 Track brake cooling duct
34 Gearbox
35 Track brake
36 Oil pressure pump
37 Batteries

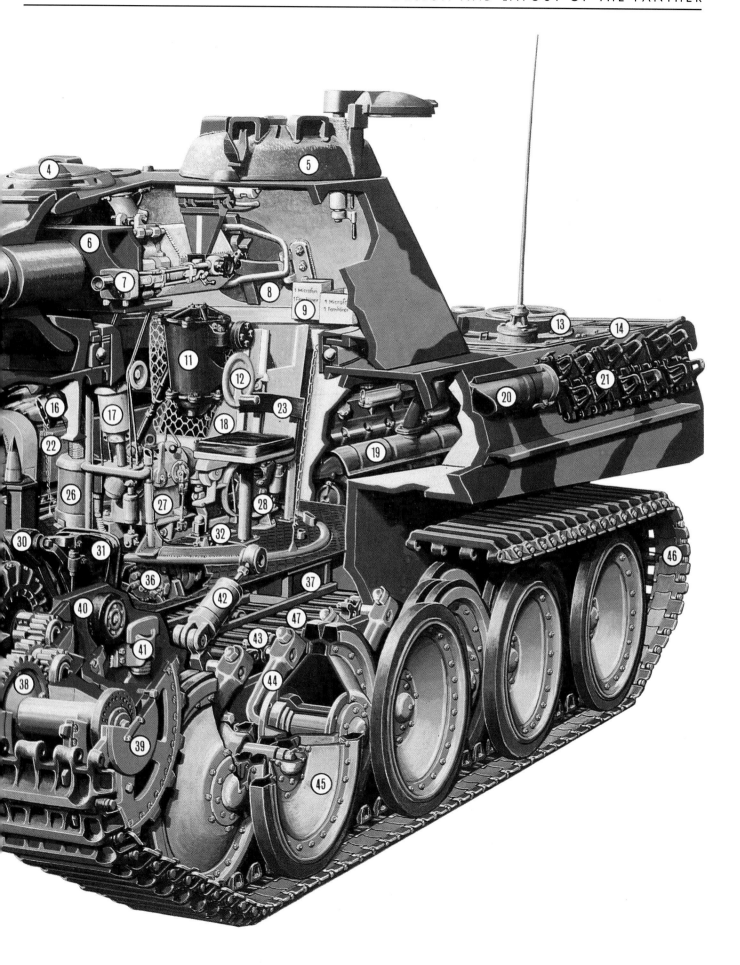

of their VK 2001 (K) which would mount either a Maybach, HL 116 or HL 115 motor, armed with a 5cm gun, and 50mm- (1.97in-) thick frontal armour. That October, Krupp received contracts for three VK 2001 (K)s from Wa Prüf 6. Krupp also produced a heavier design, the VK 2301 (K). However, neither the Daimler-Benz nor the Krupp designs were fitted with the torsion bar suspension system which Kniepkamp wanted. Therefore, he turned to MAN and MAN completed layout drawings of a VK 2001 (M) with interleaved wheels and torsion bar suspension in October 1940. Consequently, Wa Prüf 6 awarded them with a contract to design an improved version, the VK 2002 (M). This was to have six 180mm (7.09in) road wheels, torsion bar suspension, and a Maybach HL 90 motor. The hull would have 50mm (1.97in)

Below: The pistol port on this Ausf D is visible on the side of the turret below a non-standard container, typical of the sort of modifications made by tank crews in the field.

front plates and 40mm (1.57in) side and rear armour protection. In response to the success of sloped armour on Soviet tanks which the Wehrmacht was now meeting on the Eastern Front, MAN redesigned the hull for the VK 2002 (M) with sloping armour in November 1941. Despite this development work, none of the companies expected to win large-scale contracts for production of a battle tank from their VK 20 designs. On its past performance, the PzKpfw IV had appeared to be perfectly adequate for the Wehrmacht's needs.

Events on the Eastern Front, however, had a drastic effect on German tank development. The PzKpfw IV was shown to be inferior to the T-34 and a replacement was desperately needed. Rather than putting extra effort into the VK 20 programme, a whole new weight and class of tank was deemed necessary, a decision made against the advice of Wa Prüf 6. Armaments Reichminister Fritz Todt had declared that a 30.5-tonne (30-ton) tank must be designed and put into produc-

tion. The head of the organisation, Colonel Fichtner, believed this was misguided and claimed on 17 December 1941 that 'in his opinion, time would be lost since the 30-ton tank had yet to be developed'. Fichtner advocated persevering with the VK 20-based designs as development of many of the models neared completion. Furthermore, a heavier tank would mean less were produced and many firms were in no position to build a 30.5-tonne (30-ton) design. With regard to the new tank's deployment in the field, Wehrmacht engineer bridges could not take the weight of such a vehicle, nor could most of Europe's road bridges. Thus a tank of such weight would depend on submerged river crossing, a problem which the Germans had not adequately solved. Unsurprisingly, it was Todt, not Fichtner, who prevailed.

GUDERIAN'S PANZER COMMISSION

In response to Guderian's demands for a new tank to beat the T-34, a special Panzer Commission was dispatched to the

Colonel-General's Panzer Army to gain first-hand knowledge of the situation the German tank crews faced. Many of Guderian's men could provide a simple solution to the problem: 'The officers at the front were of the opinion that the the T-34 should simply be copied, since this would be the quickest way of putting to rights the most unhappy situation of the German panzer troops.' It was, of course, not quite so simple. Some commentators have suggested that the German decision not to copy directly the T-34 was based on racial reasons: the German designers could not bring themselves to make a direct copy of a tank built by a supposedly inferior race. This is not strictly accurate. As Guderian himself points out, 'It would not be possible to mass-produce essential elements of the T-34 – in particular the aluminium diesel engines – with the necessary speed. Also, so far as steel alloys went, we were at a disadvantage compared to the Russians, owing to our shortage of raw materials.' Even so, the subsequent German design of the Panther owed much to its Soviet adversary. Nonetheless, there were extremely different philosophies at work in the design of Soviet and German tanks. For one thing, the designers of the T-34 gave little consideration to the comfort of their tanks' crew. The interior was rough and simple, but this was considered suitable for the hardy Soviet tank men. In contrast, Guderian attached great importance to the comfort and convenience of his crews and, in the early days, had demanded that they should be selected with the same care that the Luftwaffe chose its air crews. The PzKpfw III and IV had five-man crews, one more than their Soviet, French and British contemporary designs. This ensured that the crew were not overworked. The German tanks were also comfortable to ride in and were highly complex machines. Such a design and operational philosophy was never likely to produce an exact copy of the crude but effective T-34.

The commission was headed by Fichtner of Wa Prüf 6 and consisted of German industry and Wa Prüf 6's most important designers, including Kniepkamp and Major Ruden of Wa Prüf 6, Professor Doctor Ferdinand Porsche, and representatives of Steyr, Vereinigte Stahlwerke, Daimler-Benz, Krupp, Henschel, MAN and Rheinmetall. They arrived at Guderian's headquarters on 18 November 1941 and Guderian greeted them with a speech which outlined some of the problems they faced. Throughout the campaigns of Poland and France, and the early days in Russia, he claimed, German tanks had been superior to those of their enemies. Now the situation was different. Guderian told the commission, 'The purpose of the new equipment should be to re-establish the previous superiority.' In the Soviet Union, the Germans had encountered all manner of difficult terrain. In the summer, the dust in an 'unexpected quantity' had damaged engines. In the autumn, mud had been encountered on the unimproved roads, as well as in the countryside. Vehicles had become bogged down and so, obviously, what was required was an improvement in the ground pressure exerted by German

Above: A close-up of the Panther's turret showing the Zimmerit anti-magnetic mine paste. The Fu 8 radio antennae behind the commander's cupola indicates this to be a *Befehlswagen* Command Panther.

tanks. In the winter, tank tracks slipped in the icy conditions and the cold had made the metal brittle. This was quite apart from the freezing temperatures and the driving snow the Germans had yet to encounter. The T-34 and KV I had proved largely impervious to German weapons. Thus, Guderian wanted 'a new gun that can penetrate the Russian tanks at a range where they cannot penetrate ours'. The 76.2mm (3in) tank gun employed by the Soviets was the most effective weapon on the Eastern Front and so the Germans needed thicker armour. However, Guderian was also determined that any new tank designs should have 'improved suspension with wider tracks ... and a more powerful motor ... Particular attention is to be paid to maintaining a high horsepower to weight ratio. The ability to drive cross-country and on unimproved trails in all seasons must be made possible.'

The Panzer Commission visited a tank repair company where they were presented with proposals for improvements in the air filters and heaters of German tanks to keep out the clogging Russian dust. They talked to engineering officers, visited recent battle fields, inspected Russian tanks and met tank repair- and recovery crews from the 14th Panzer Corps. Guderian met the Commission again on 21 November 1941 and outlined the priority in new tank designs: primarily, heavier armament; secondly, higher tactical mobility; and thirdly, improved armour protection. He stressed that by the time of the next offensive, at the least, he needed guns which could penetrate the new Soviet tanks.

A number of firms had been working on the VK 3001 specification from 1937, which was a parallel programme to the VK 2001 series. Daimler-Benz, Henschel, MAN and Porsche had all dabbled in this area. Henschel had completed four prototypes on their VK 3001 programme, two in March 1941, and two in October of the same year. The programme was scrapped on the recommendation of the Panzer committee and the four prototypes used to mount 128mm self-propelled guns. Henschel then turned to the development of a 45.7 tonne- (45-ton) vehicle capable of carrying an 88mm gun. This was the basis of the famous Tiger tank. Porsche had entered the VK 3001 programme in 1939 and, by 1940, had completed two prototypes which had been thoroughly tested. However, as a result of the Panzer Commission, Porsche soon turned its attention to the Tiger programme as well.

MAN and Daimler-Benz remained working in the area of the 30.5-tonne (30-ton) class. The two companies received contracts from Wa Prüf 6 on 25 November 1941 to develop a tank, designated VK 3002, which soon gained the name 'Panther' during its development at both MAN and Daimler-Benz. The design specifications called for a tank with 60mm (2.36in) frontal and 40mm (1.57in) side armour. Learning from the design of the T-34, this armour was to be sloped. The maximum speed was to be 55k/h (34.1m/h) and the VK 3002 should be capable of a sustained speed of 40k/h (24.9m/h). On 22 January 1942, two MAN engineers, Meyer and Wiebicke, met Colonel Fichtner, Lieutenant Colonel von Wilcke, Major Crohn and Kniepkamp of Wa Prüf 6. They were told that the combat weight of the VK 3002 had been increased to 35.6 tonnes (35 tons). They were also shown a model of the Daimler-Benz proposal which bore a strong resemblance to the T-34. As Daimler-Benz had promised to deliver their first experimental vehicle in May 1942, they agreed to deliver the MAN vehicle during the same month.

THE DAIMLER-BENZ DESIGN

Daimler-Benz produced their VK 3002 (DB) with a diesel engine. The MB 507 engine was a development of the company's M 71 aircraft engine which had been adapted for use in armoured fighting vehicles. It was an excellent design which provided higher torque and a more satisfactory torque curve and which allowed higher tractive power at lower speed ranges. As a fuel, diesel also had the advantage of considerably reducing the risk of fire. Daimler-Benz also produced a version with their MB 503 petrol engine as well as three mounting the Maybach HL 210 motor. Its suspension used leaf springs rather than torsion bars and these external leaf springs were easily accessible, thus allowing easy maintenance. Another benefit was that they permitted larger internal height, or a lower overall height. The transmission was fitted in the rear, thereby allowing a larger area for the gun. Tests were done on the VK 3001 (DB) chassis, which was already running, involving superimposed steering gears and steering controls. This hydraulic steering system made remote control possible and meant the driver could even be situated in the turret cage, if so desired. These ideas, which evolved from the VK 3001 tests, were applied to the VK 3002 (DB). The total weight of the Daimler-Benz prototype was 34.5 tonnes (34 tons) and it could reach a maximum speed of 54k/h (33.4m/h). Using a constant mesh Maybach Olvar eight-speed gearbox and controlled by multi-clutch brakes, it also employed a hydraulically operated multidisk-type clutch. The same method was used for its clutch steering. For spot turns, the inner track could be fully locked and thus the VK 3002 (DB) turned on its track. Its bogies were similar to that of the T-34 and, due to shortages, the wheels were without rubber tyres. Indeed, the whole design, as the MAN engineers had noted, looked very similar to the Soviet tank.

Daimler-Benz were rather proud of their design and felt that the VK 3002 (DB) would prove superior to the MAN tank. Indeed, Dr Kissel of the company's board of directors seems to have believed that he had convinced Reichminister Todt of this. In February 1942, he wrote to one of his colleagues that 'you will greatly enjoy hearing that it was possible to convince the Reichminister that a decision in favour of our new proposed tank is the correct one. When this decision is reached, the gentlemen from both the *Heereswaffenamt* [Army Ordnance Department] and MAN will indeed be astonished.' The staff of Wa Prüf 6 were somewhat annoyed by this apparent preference for the Daimler-Benz. MAN engineers Wiebicke and Reif reported that 'Kniepkamp [of Wa Prüf 6] was very put out over this matter.'

At this crucial stage Todt was killed in a plane crash in February 1942 and was succeeded by Albert Speer. However Speer also appeared to favour the Daimler-Benz tank, as he reported on 5 March 1942 that:

'On my recommendation, Hitler ordered that contracts be awarded for any preparations necessary to develop a series of Daimler-Benz Panzers and to give Daimler-Benz a contract for a series of 200. Hitler considered the Daimler-Benz Panther to be superior to the MAN Panther. Considering the various differences in design, Hitler believed that in almost all cases the advantage could be given to Daimler-Benz.'

It appeared to the directors of Daimler-Benz that they had the contract pretty much in their pocket.

ARMOURED VEHICLE NOMENCLATURE

The tanks (*Panzerkampfwagen*) wth which Germany fought World War II were intially abbreviated as 'PzKw', but this caused confusion, since personnel carriers were known by the abbreviation 'PKw'. Armoured fighting vehicles thus came to be designated 'PzKpfw' or 'Pz.Kpfw', though not until halfway through the war. A Roman numeral was used to distinguish one vehicle type from another – PzKpfw IV, for example – and models or versions were distinguished by a capital letter alphabetic *Ausführung* number, usually abbreviated to Ausf.

In addition, all vehicles of the German armed services received a unique SdKfz (*Sonderkraftfahrzeug* – special purpose vehicle) number, which did not change from one version to the next. Thus, all 12 versions of the PzKpw III were known as SdKfz 141. The number only changed if a major variant was produced.

The last three German tanks of World War II also received names – Tiger, Panther and Tiger II. Thus they became, for example, PzKpfw V Panther Ausf G. Some tanks' designations were later changed retroactively – the PzKpfw VI Tiger Ausf H was later designated as the PzKpfw VI Tiger I Ausf E, for example. The Ausf. designators were not always alphabetical, nor did they use all the letters of the alphabet. In the case of the Panther, there were a few Ausf. As built (later reclassifed), Ausf. Bs and Cs were never put into service, Ausf. D was the first major production variant, Ausf. A the second and the final variant was the Ausf. G. Subvariants sometimes received an Arabic numeral after the alphabetic designator: PzKpfw IV Ausf. F2, for example.

Tanks of the same type but with different guns were differentiated by a reference to the main weapon. Any unique sub-designator was used, as long as it assisted vehicle identification.

From 1938, prototype and experimental tanks first received a 'VK' (*Vollkettenkraftfahrzeug* – full-tracked motor vehicle) designator, followed by a four-digit number, the first pair of which described its weight in tonnes, while the second pair differentiated one prototype from another. When an identical specification was given to two or more manufacturers, a simple abbreviation of their name was appended, in brackets: VK 3001 (H) for example, for a Henschel tank. From 1943 experimental tanks got a simpler 'E' (*Entwicklungstyp* – development type) designation, followed by an approximate weight-class.

THE MAN DESIGN

Although the MAN Panther design will be examined in considerable detail in the second half of this chapter, in looking at the layout of the tank, it is worth noting some of the salient features of the MAN VK 3002 (M) to give an idea of the choice which confronted the special commission set up to decide between the MAN and Daimler-Benz designs.

The MAN design was well shaped, and also learnt the lesson of the advantages of sloping armour from the T-34. However, it was too heavy and its profile too high to be a true medium tank replacement for the PzKpfw IV. The constant modification which had taken place through the design process had taken the weight from 35.5 tonnes (35 tons) to 43.7 tonnes (43 tons). The engine for the VK 3002 (M) was initially a Maybach HL 210, although this was not considered powerful enough. The MAN Panther actually used twin torsion bar suspension for its eight interleaved road wheels, a Zahnradfabrik AK 7/200 transmission, and a clutch brake steering gear.

Below: From front to rear, a Panther, American Grant and Tiger mount an obstacle in Italy. The tanks are probably involved in a comparative trial or training exercise.

THE CHOICE BETWEEN MAN AND DAIMLER-BENZ

Hitler appointed a special commission consisting of Colonel Thomale of Inspektorate 6, responsible for tank procurement, and Professor Doctor of Engineering von Eberan from the Technical College of Dresden, to review the designs and recommend which Panther should go into large-scale production. The commission turned the early preference for the Daimler-Benz design on its head. The report of 11 May 1942 was unanimously in favour of the MAN design and this decision was passed on to the chairman of the Panzer Commission. The special commission felt that Daimler-Benz had been sorely lacking in its provision for a turret on their Panther design as the company's own proposal for a turret was incomplete and would thus delay production until December 1942. The turret ring diameter was 50mm (1.97in) narrower than the MAN design, which meant that it could not fit the Rheinmetall turret which had been prepared in parallel with the Daimler-Benz and MAN designs. Rheinmetall-Borsig had received a contract in July 1941 to produce a 7.5cm tank gun and turret for the VK 3002 designs. Thus, the Daimler-Benz Panther chassis had no available turret. According to the commission, the MAN Panther suspension provided a better gun platform. Its motor com-

partment allowed submersion in water without lengthy preparation, which might prove vital, given the problem of finding bridges capable of taking a tank of this weight. Its design, coupled with the Maybach engine, gave the vehicle a longer range. Hitler was shown the commission's report on 13 May 1942, and he reckoned that the armour was too weak, but otherwise approved of the commission's findings, officially making his decision the following day after studying the report overnight. He certainly recognised that getting the design into production as soon as possible was the key to the issue. In fact, Hitler agreed fully with the special commission's recommendations and, given this backing at the highest level, it was the MAN Panther that was to enter production. On 15 May 1942, Fichtner of Wa Prüf 6 telephoned MAN and informed the company of the Führer's decision. The development of the Daimler-Benz Panther immediately ceased.

The Daimler-Benz board of directors met on 3 June 1942 to discuss why they had lost to MAN. They consoled themselves that initially, many experts had sided with their proposal, and that 'even Hitler had expressed his approval'. However, Thomale and Eberan considered that the Daimler-Benz design was inferior for the following reasons: their design had used leaf spring suspension, whereas the double torsion bar system was preferred. Furthermore, the commission considered that the MB 507 engine could not be produced easily and quickly enough to the extent required. However, the key problem was the turret. The Daimler-Benz required a new turret design; the MAN vehicle had a turret already prepared.

On 4 June 1942, Hitler demanded that the frontal armour on the Panther be increased even further. The increase to 80mm (3.15in) that he had requested in May, he now considered insufficient. He wanted all frontal vertical surfaces of the tank to have a 100mm- (3.9in) thick armour. On that same day, a meeting was held between the four companies who would produce the VK 3002 Panther design: MAN; Daimler-Benz; Henschel; and MNH. Its purpose was to agree on standardised production. MAN also received the contract to produce an experimental chassis by August, and a tank complete with turret by September 1942, a contract which it met that autumn. The first of the Versuchs-Panther Fgst Nr V1 was an experimental chassis – without turret – completed in September. As it did not have a turret, it carried out its trials bearing a test weight to compensate. Along with its twin, the Fgst Nr V2 (complete with turret), it satisfactorily demonstrated its automotive performance at driving trials at Berka near Eisenbach between 8–14 November 1942. Speer and Wa Prüf 6 were happy enough with these designs to award an initial order for 1000 Panther Ausf Ds (as the first production model was called) with MAN, Daimler-Benz, Henschel and MNH, and the new tank was designated the PzKpfw V Panther. Once taken into service, it was given the SdKfz (*Sonderkraftfahrzeug* – special purposes vehicle)

Above: A frontal view of the Panther Ausf D, which can be distinguished by the slot on the left for the radio operator's machine gun. For comparison, an Ausf G is visible in the background.

number 171, in order to distinguish it in German ordnance vocabulary, a number which remained constant through the Ausf D, A and G models. Only variants differing considerably from the standard model were given a different SdKfz number, such as the *Panzerbefehlswagen* Panther command tanks, designated SdKfz 267 and 268, and the *Bergepanther* armoured recovery vehicle, designated SdKfz 179.

LAYOUT OF THE PZKPFW V 'PANTHER'

The layout of the Panther was fairly conventional by World War II standards and conformed to the usual pattern of German tanks. The driving and transmission compartments were situated forward, the fighting compartment and turret were in the middle, and the engine compartment was located at the rear. The internal positions of the crew also followed the standard German layout. The driver and hull gunner/wireless operator sat in the front compartment and the main gunner, loader, and commander all had stations in the

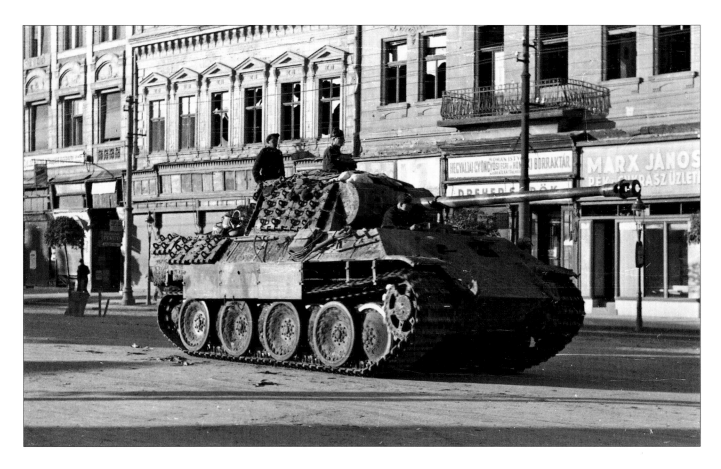

Above: Spare pieces of track have been attached to this Panther to provide further protection against anti-tank weapons. Some of the *Schürzen* skirts on the side of the tank have been torn away.

turret. As in all German tanks, the crew were placed close together. This close proximity had the considerable morale benefit of providing reassurance and allowed communication by touch – or lip reading, if necessary – in the noise and confusion of battle. They could also cooperate easily in emergencies, such as the wounding of a colleague, jammed guns or provision of ammunition.

THE CHASSIS AND SUSPENSION

The chassis mounted eight sets of interleaved road wheels (or bogies) on either side. The road wheels were carried on twin torsion bars lying transversely across the tank. The outboard end of the arm mounted the suspension wheel. The inboard end was connected by a swinging link to another torsion bar whose other end was secured to the tank side. This hairpin shaped bar provided double its length and avoided the need to use longitudinal bars to provide the necessary combination of response to shocks associated by normal driving conditions, whilst giving sufficient stiffness to withstand abnormal blows. This system gave the Panther the best designed suspension of any German tank. Furthermore, its lateral installation in the tank meant it was well protected by its armour, although the system took up useful space within the armour envelope and increased the tank's weight.

Each axle mounted a road wheel set made up of two tyred discs, arranged in pairs. The outer and inner 'discs' were spaced close together on the one axle and – due to the interleaved arrangement of the Panther's wheels – spaced widely on the alternate axle, allowing the edge of the closely spaced wheel to sit slightly between them. The pattern was repeated down the length of the tank. The interleaved overlapping wheel system meant more suspension units could be installed. thus improving the smoothness of the ride and also providing a more uniform load distribution over the tracks than other, more conventional, arrangements. While it was theoretically attractive in practice mud, slush and snow could pack between the wheels, which would prove particularly serious in the harsh Russian winter as the build of debris could freeze solid, thereby jamming the interleaved pairs of wheels. From a maintenance point of view, one of the biggest disadvantages of this arrangement was the fact that the removal of one inside wheel necessitated the removal of four others.

The road wheels themselves were 860mm (33.9in)in diameter and had rubber tyres. From September 1944, MAN installed steel road wheels with internal rubber cushioning on a limited number Ausf Gs. These wheels were the same as those mounted on some Tiger Is and all King Tiger IIs. Steel tyred wheels were also installed on the final station on some of the last Ausf Gs turned out by MAN in March–April 1945. It is not clear if this was due to a rubber shortage or if it was intended as a design improvement. The suspension system was completed by a pair of front drive sprockets and rear idlers – which also acted as tensioning wheels for the track – two hydraulic shock absorbers, and a return roller each side. To simplify production, the rear shock absorbers were removed from Ausf G tanks after October 1944. This made little difference to the smoothness of the Panther's cross-country ride. Over this system rode the Panther's tracks. The unlubricated manganese steel skeleton track's 86 links were held together by a single pin and designated Kgs 64/660/160, meaning that the tracks were 660mm (26in) wide and the distance between the link pins was 160mm (6.3in). The tracks had been designed for the 35.5 tonne- (35-ton) prototype and were not widened for the heavier combat model. Nonetheless, this provided the Ausf D with the very reasonable ground pressure of 0.723kg (1.6lb) per cm2 for such a heavy vehicle. The ground pressure of the Ausf A and G was 0.9kg (1.98lb) and 0.8kg (1.76lb) per cm2 respectively. In September 1943, a new track link design was introduced which was fitted with chevroned cleats intended to increase traction and reduce slipping in icy conditions and on surfaces such as cobblestones. On the Ausf A, ice sprags were issued to units as part of their winter equipment. These sprags were fitted on every fifth to seventh track link to improve performance on snow covered roads. When fitted, it was advisable not to exceed the speed of 15k/h (9.32m/h).

THE HULL AND ARMOUR

Up until 1942, German tanks were basically square in shape. The front and side armoured plate were at right angles to the ground. The designers of the Panther, however, had learnt from the sloped armour used on the T-34. They knew that sloping armour gave excellent ballistic protection and accordingly the glacis plate was sloped specifically to defect shells upwards and clear of the mantlet. The glacis plate was 80mm (3.14in) thick and sloped at 55 degrees. The sides were 40mm (1.57in) thick but vertical, and the rear 40mm (1.57in) thick at 30 degrees, whereas the roof was 16mm (0.63in) thick and the belly between 16mm (0.63in) and 30mm (1.18in) thick. The hull and superstructure was a single, built-up unit of thick, well-sloped homogeneous rolled armour plate of welded construction. The armour was softer than earlier and thinner homogeneous armour, and no face-hardening was employed. However, the size and weight caused problems, so to overcome this, plates of the largest possible size were used. The armoured plates were designed to interlock and a special step cut in the joints to make a

Below: American infantry inspect a knocked-out Panther in Normandy in 1944. The eight large, interleaving road wheels for the track to run on can clearly be seen.

seating for the welds. Considerable attention was paid to the integrity of those welded joints, both to increase the rigidity of the hull as a whole, and also to improve protection from incoming fire. The technique of interlocking 'much in the manner of a woodworker's cross-halving or mortise and tenon joint' produced less stress in the joints than simple juxtaposition welds. Austenitic, electro-arc welding was used, which completed the joint in a single pass and produced a truly homogeneous union. This provided the tank with a considerable degree of protection.

The Panther was impenetrable to the Sherman A2, British Cromwell and Churchill – all armed with the 75mm M3 gun – at any range from the front. The Sherman A4, with a 76mm M1 A1 gun, and the T-34/85, armed with an 85mm S53 gun, could only penetrate the turret armour from the front. Success against the Panther generally required a shot against the sides or rear. The angle of the upper wall of the hull on the Panther Ausf G was reduced from 40 degrees to 29 degrees. In order to maintain the equivalent protection, the wall thickness was increased from 40mm (1.57in) to 50mm (1.96in). From April 1943, Schürzen (protective side skirts)

Below: A Panther crew work on their camouflaged tank, which is being moved to the front on a flatbed rail truck. The tank's tracks were so wide that it had to be carefully positioned in transit.

were mounted. These skirts were made of mild steel plates 5mm (0.19in) thick and were designed to protect the tank from rounds fired at close range by Russian anti-tank rifles. They also were effective against hits from 75mm high-explosive shells. Although not designed for this purpose, the Schürzen provided useful protection against hollow charge (HEAT) projectiles by exploding the shells away from the body of the tank and dispersing the jet stream before it hit the tank. In September 1943, *Zimmerit* (anti-magnetic coating) was applied on every new Ausf D at the factory to all the upright surfaces which could be reached by a man standing on the ground. Its purpose was to prevent the use of magnetic anti-tank grenades. This nitro-solvent based Zimmerit was rippled to increase the distance on the steel surface without increasing the weight of the coating. However, in September 1944 Wa Prüf 6 ordered that the application of Zimmerit to Ausf Gs should cease, largely to cut down on the man hours it took to apply the coating, as well as the six days required for the filler to dry. At a time when every tank was needed at the front, these days were crucial.

THE ENGINE

The engine was housed in the rear of the hull and was flanked on each side by cooling radiators and extractor fans. As with all German tanks – except the PzKpfw 1A which had

a 60 horsepower Krupp engine – the Panther used engines, designed by Maybach Motorenbau GmbH of Friedrichshafen, and built by Maybach and Nordbau of Berlin. According to the British War Office, 'This Maybach monopoly was no doubt due to the friendship between Doctor Maybach and Kniepkamp of Wa Prüf 6.' All the same, this Maybach monopoly was slightly unfortunate. While the engines were good, they were extremely complicated, especially in the powerful version fitted to the Panther. Skilled drivers could get the best out of them, but the supply of such men dwindled as the war progressed. The engine originally planned for the Panther was the Maybach HL210 P30, and this was installed on the first 250 Ausf D tanks. It produced 650 horsepower at 3000 revolutions per minute (rpm). This, however, was considered underpowered. As the Panther was considerably heavier than its intended original weight, a more powerful engine was necessary. Therefore, the HL210 was replaced with the HL230 P30. This was basically the same engine, but its capacity was raised from 21 litres (4.61 gallons) to 23 litres (5.05 gallons) by enlarging the cylinder bore. This left virtually no space between adjacent cylinder liners. The HL 230 P30 was a short V12 cylinder wate-cooled petrol engine with four solex carburettors. The engine weighed 1300kg (2866lb) and rested on a cast-iron engine block. The HL230 P30 produced 700 horsepower at

3000rpm; this had to be limited to 2500rpm in service. Although this did not increase the speed of the Panther overall, it did allow the Panther to accelerate faster, climb slopes quicker, and cross difficult terrain with less strain on the engine. It produced a power-to-weight ratio of 15.6 horsepower per tonne in the Ausf G. The Panther's maximum road speed was pretty good at 46km/h (28.74m/h) and 24km/h (14.9m/h) cross country. Its road range was 170km (105.6 miles) and 89km (55.3 miles) cross country.

The HL230 P30 was also fitted with two newly designed air filters which ducted the incoming air through an oil bath. This successfully captured 99 per cent of contaminating particles. The exhaust was taken away through manifolds through two exhaust pipes on the rear protected by cast, and later welded, armour guards. From June 1944, sheet metal covers were fitted to the sides of the exhaust pipes as a measure to hide the tell-tale glow given off at night when the pipes were hot. The Maybach engine used an eight-bearing crank shaft that barely fitted into the small engine compartment. Access to the engine was via a large inspection hatch in the rear decking.

Below: American infantry being briefed on the Panther tank, a formidable opponent for all Allied tanks and personnel. The escape hatch is open on the turret rear.

Above: An array of German armour late in the war. From front to rear: a StuG IV assault gun, a Panther and a Pzkpfw IV panzer. The driver's vision slot is open on the Panther.

The engine was situated at the rear of the tank and drove forward via a shaft beneath the turret floor to the gear box situated between the driver and wireless operator, with a final drive which led each side to the front sprockets.

THE DRIVER AND HIS CONTROLS

The driver sat in the left-hand forward position with the gearbox to the right. The Panther had a conventional mechanical transmission. A subsidiary of Maybach, the Zahnradfabrik of Friedrichshafen, produced the AK7-200 gearbox. It was a hand-operated syncro-mesh design which provided seven speeds forward and one reverse. The gearbox with clutch and crown wheel weighed 750kg (1653lb). An LAG 3/70 H dry clutch was fitted. As the Panther differed radically from preceding German tanks, a new steering gear and steering brakes were developed by MAN. The driver steered in the conventional manner operating the Argus disc brakes hydraulically by breaking the tracks. However, the epicyclic gears could also be used to assist steering. Driving the direct gear of the epicyclic via the steering clutch against the direction of the main drive retarded the track on that side. The vehicle could travel in each gear through a curve of a fixed radius. Thus, the system was described as a single radius steering gear. The driver could see forwards through a vision port in front of him in the glacis plate and the port was fitted with a laminated glass screen. Its armoured hinged flap, positioned on the outside, was closed in combat. Under these circumstances, forward vision was provided by two fixed episcopes, one facing forwards and the other to the left

front at a 10.30 position. This provided a rather restricted view and was replaced with a pivoting traversable periscope, resulting in the deletion of the driver's visor and providing a smooth glacis plate on the driver's side.

THE HULL GUNNER/RADIO OPERATOR

The hull gunner/radio operator sat on the right side forward. On the early Ausf D models, he fired his 7.92mm MG 34 machine gun through a letterbox shaped hatch in the glacis plate in front of him. This somewhat unsatisfactory arrangement was replaced by an armoured integral ball mounting which held the MG 34. He could traverse his machine gun 5 degrees to the left and 5 degrees to the right and had a vertical arc of -10 degrees/+15 degrees. On the Ausf D, his vision was provided by two fixed periscopes on the roof above his head, allowing a view towards the front and right front. On the Ausf A and G, the gunner's episcopes were deleted as he used the KZF2 (Kugelzielfernrohr – ball mounting sighting telescope) sight provided with the new machine gun mount for observation. The cranked monocular sight provided magnification of x1.75 and a field of vision of 18 degrees. The radio equipment was located to his right on a sponson which overhung the tracks. All Panthers were fitted with a single FuG 5 radio set. It had a 10-watt transmitter, a short-wave receiver, and operated in the 27,200-3,300Mhz frequency band. Its range varied from between 4-6km (2.5-3.7 miles), depending on terrain and atmospheric conditions. The set provided an intercom system for the crew. Access to the driver and hull gunner/radio operator positions were by twin hatches above their positions in the hull. As these hatches were often blocked, depending on the turret traverse, jettisonable hatches were installed so the driver and hull gunner/radio operator could escape quickly in an emergency.

THE TURRET

The 8.12-tonne (8-ton) turret had sloped walls and a rounded front which mounted a curved cast armour gun mantlet. The turret's front plate and side plate were interlocked using a dovetail joint on the Ausf D and a squared off joint on the Ausf A and G, making manufacturing simpler. The front plate was 100mm (3.93in) thick, set at 12 degrees, and the mantlet was also 100mm (3.93in) thick. The side and rear were 45mm (1.77in) thick at 25 degrees and the roof 16mm (0.62in) thick. The original mantlet had a tendency to deflect armoured piercing rounds, striking the lower half of it downwards, sometimes penetrating the roof of the hull and, at other times, directing rounds on to the vulnerable turret ring. A chingun mantlet, designed to deflect projectiles upwards, was introduced on the Ausf G from September 1944 onwards. The turret cage had a full floor which rotated with the turret. It was driven from the main shaft which lay between two half shafts and was mounted in a housing which worked the turret drive.

TURRET CREW

The vehicle's commander sat at the left rear of the turret. This offset location was necessitated by the length of the breech of the KwK 42 gun which virtually divided the turret compartment in two. On the first three models, it was discovered that the commander's right side was in serious danger of being hit by the recoiling gun. Initially, a guard had to be fitted to protect his right arm and right knee but his seat was soon redesigned so as to avoid the gun's recoil. In German tanks, the commander's role was purely the direction of the crew and tank and observation of the terrain. He was less overburdened than his Soviet counterpart in the T-34/76 who also had to aim and fire the tank's main armament. The Panther commander had to be provided with excellent viewing devices. This was the prominent 'dustbin' type cupola with six vision slits on the Ausf D. During the rebuilds of Ausf D Panthers at the Demag plant at Falkensee, a mount for the TSR 1 observation periscope was fitted to the commander's cupola. The TSR 1 allowed the commander to observe the terrain, even from turret-down positions. On the Ausf A, a new cupola was installed, made of a cast armour insert with seven episcopes protected by armoured cowlings. A sighting vein was also positioned in front of the cupola for the commander to line up targets for the gunner. He also had a traverse indicator marked in clock hours from 1 to 12 on a ring in the cupola. The cupola hatch opened horizontally. An anti-aircraft machine-gun ring was often fitted to mount an MG 34. In addition to his access to the radio set, the commander also had flag sets and a signal pistol.

Below: Twin exhaust ports were standard on the Panther. The rear hatch on the turret was usually used for loading the 75mm (2.95in) ammunition, but it also served as an escape hatch.

PzKpfw V Panther Ausf D

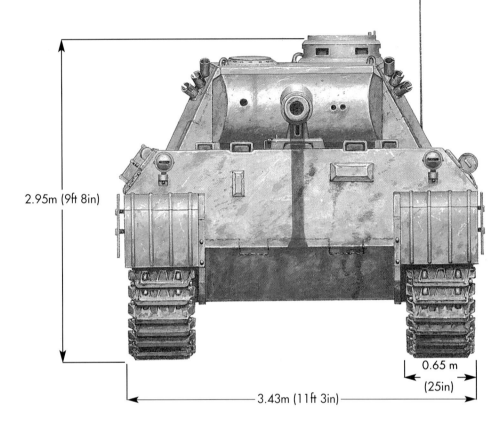

2.95m (9ft 8in)

0.65 m
(25in)

3.43m (11ft 3in)

8.86m (29ft)

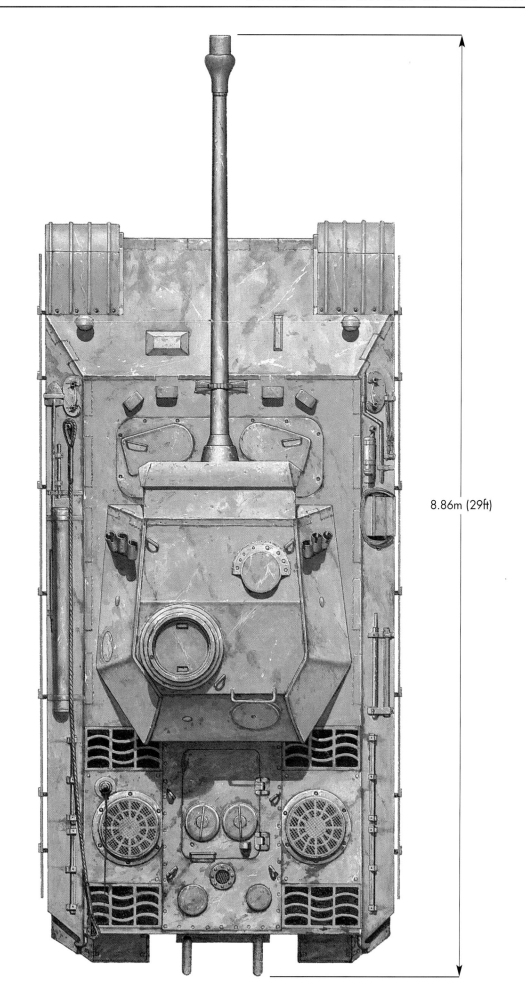

8.86m (29ft)

Above: The 75mm (2.95in) long-barrelled gun of the Panther could be depressed further than that of the T-34. This gave the Panther an advantage when fighting in 'hull-down' defensive positions.

The gunner sat on the left-hand side of the main armament. He sighted the gun through a Leitz TzF 12 binocular articulated sighting telescope with a stationary eye piece and moving illuminated graticles which provided x 2.5 magnification. In late November and early December 1943, this was replaced by the TzF 12a monocular sight. This provided x2.5 magnification and a field of view of 28 degrees, used for target acquisition, and x5 magnification with a reduced field of view of 14 degrees for accurate gun laying at long range. The adjustable range scales allowed the gunner to gauge the exact distance to the target. It also had a range scale graduated in hundreds of metres out to 2000m (6561ft) for the Pzgr 40/42 special anti-tank round, 3000m (9842ft) for the Pzgr 39/42 standard armour piercing shell, and 4000m (13,123ft) for the high explosive Sprgr 42. The gunner, like the commander, was also provided with a traverse indicator. He fired the gun electrically by a trigger fitted to the elevating handwheel and fired the coaxial machine gun by a foot pedal on the turret floor. The loader sat to the right of the KwK 42 cannon and was also responsible for the loading and maintenance of the coaxial machine gun. He was provided with an observation episcope from the Ausf A onwards.

The Ausf D turret was rotated by a hydraulic motor which traversed the turret at a maximum speed of 360 degrees in

60 seconds, independent of the engine speed. An improved system was fitted to the Ausf A, whereby the speed of turret traverse was dependent on engine speed. At the maximum engine speed of 3000rpm, it traversed at a maximum rate of 360 degrees in 15 seconds. However, after November 1943, when the Maybach HL 230 P30 was limited to 2500rpm, the turret traverse speed decreased to a maximum of 360 degrees in 18 seconds. The hydraulic traverse allowed rapid target acquisition. However, fine adjustment was achieved by use of the gunner's hand traverse and hand elevation wheels. If the power failed, the gunner could traverse the turret manually, assisted by the loader's use of an auxiliary hand traverse. The main armament's elevation was -8 degrees to +18 degrees. Turret openings were kept to a minimum. Access for the driver was through a hatch on the front right of the roof, and for the commander through his cupola. A large circular hatch on the rear face provided access for the loader and was also used for ammunitioning. On the left-hand side, beneath the cupola, there was a small communication port. This is often mistaken for a spent cartridge ejection port but it appears, in fact, to have been used for communication between the tank commander and accompanying infantry. It was deleted after July 1943. There are also pistol ports on the left and right and rear of the turret, through which the crew's small arms could be fired. These were replaced when the *Nahverteidigungswaffe* (close defence weapon) was installed on the Ausf A from March 1944 onwards. Their fitting was by no means uniform.

THE MAIN ARMAMENT

'Armour and movement are only two of the combat characteristics of the tank weapon; the third and the most important is fire-power.' Heinz Guderian

German tank designers had long realised that it was impossible to guarantee completely the protection of tanks against anti-tank weaponry. They believed that the gun would always beat the armour and therefore they concentrated on tank armament as the most important factor of any tank they produced. The whole story of German tank armament was one of continuous increases in calibre, the weight of shell, and barrel length and, consequently, muzzle velocity. All of these factors resulted in greater penetration of enemy tanks at longer ranges. As a general rule, German tank armament was usually well in advance of Allied, particularly Western Allied, development. On 18 July 1941, Rheinmetall-Borsig received a contract to develop a tank gun that would be able to penetrate 140mm (5.51in) of armour at 1000m (3280ft). At the same time the company was also authorised to design a turret for the VK 3002 project which would be able to take such a gun.

Their starting point was the very successful PaK 40 anti-tank gun which had been adapted to fit the PzKpfw IV as the KwK 40. The KwK 40 was a 7.5cm weapon of L/48 (48 cali-

Above: Panther turrets on a production line in a bombed factory that has been overrun by the Allies. Panther turrets were used in their own right as anti-tank guns in fixed defensive positions.

bres) length which had been adapted to take a short-necked cartridge case instead of the long-barrelled side case of its anti-tank gun cousin. The KwK 40 was an excellent gun but Rheinmetall knew that they needed something better, particularly given Hitler's preference for large calibre tank armament. At the beginning of 1942, they therefore conducted test firings with a barrel of 60 calibres length which nearly reached the required specifications. The barrel was then lengthened to 70 calibres and the improved version was delivered for tests in June 1942. It was judged satisfactory and placed into production to provide the main armament for the Panther.

The 7.5cm KwK 42 L/70 rifled cannon was fired by electric primer. Its recoil gear consisted of hydraulic buffer and hydro-pneumatic recuperator. It had semi-automatic breech operation with spring opening and closing, and vertical wedge breech locks. The balance of the gun was achieved artificially by a hydro-pneumatic cylinder. The gun was fitted with a muzzle brake to shorten recoil. It used the kinetic energy of the gases produced by the propellant burning, leaving the muzzle after the shell, to apply forward pull on the gun. The initial KwK 42 muzzle brake had a single chamber, although this was later increased to two, the inner chamber being replaceable. After April 1943, a barrel fumes evacuator was introduced to prevent powder gases entering the fighting compartment. These gases had had a serious effect on the crew, causing often incapacitating injury to their eyes and throats.

The KwK 42 was a superb anti-tank gun and extremely accurate, quite capable of first-time hits at ranges over 1000m (3280ft). Early reports mentioned a kill of a T-34 at a range of 3000m (9842ft). During controlled tests, it could hit a target 2m (6.56ft) high by 2.5m (8.2ft) wide, using the Pzgr 39/42 round 100 per cent of the time out to 1500m (4921ft). This dropped to 92 per cent at 2000m (6561ft) and 55 per

ARMOUR PENETRATION OF KWK 42		
(Armour plate set at 30 degrees)		
Ammunition Type	Pzgr 39/42	Pzgr 40/42
Weight	6.8kg (14.91lb)	4.75kg (10.4lb)
Velocity	935m (3067ft)/sec	1120m (3674ft)/sec
Range		
100m (328ft)	138mm (5.43in)	194mm (7.63in)
500m (1640ft)	124mm (4.88in)	174mm (6.85in)
1000m (3280ft)	111mm (4.37in)	149mm (5.86in)
1500m (4921ft)	99mm (3.89in)	127mm (5.00in)
2000m (6561ft)	89mm (3.50in)	106mm (4.17in)

cent at 3000m (9842ft). During practice, an actual gunner – allowing for variations in guns and ammunition – could achieve hits on this target 97 per cent of the time out to 1000m (3280ft), 49 per cent of the time out to 2000m (6561ft), and 18 per cent of the time at 3000m (9842ft). These levels of accuracy do not reflect the actual probability of hitting under battlefield conditions where errors of estimating range, movement, and stress meant that the probability of a first round hit was far lower. Nonetheless, an average gunner might well achieve hit percentages similar to those in practice with his second shot after observing the tracer from the first round.

THE RHEINMETALL MG 34M MACHINE GUN

Calibre	7.92mm (0.303in)
Weight	11.56kg (25.5lb)
Length	103.5cm (40.75in)
Muzzle Velocity	769.6m (2525ft) /sec
Cyclic Rate of Fire	785rpm
Feed	150 round belts
Cooling	air
Sight	cranked monocular KzF2 – Mag x 1.75

ARMOUR PENETRATION

The KwK 42's armour penetration capabilities were equally impressive. Its standard armoured piercing round was the Pzgr 39/42 APCBC (armoured piercing capped ballistic capped) with explosive filler and tracer. APCBC ammunition means that a ballistic cap is fitted over the hard steel-armoured piercing cap of the anti-tank projectile. The ballistic cap is long and has a pointed head fitted to the projectile to reduce air resistance in flight. In itself, the ballistic cap actually impedes penetration, but at medium and long ranges, it increases it. This is because the ballistic cap reduces de-acceleration caused by air resistance and thus the projectile maintains a higher striking velocity. The Pzgr 39 was a 6.8kg (14.9lb) shell which was fired at a muzzle velocity of 935m (3067ft) per second. Occasionally, a few rounds of Pzgr 40/42 were carried for use against the heaviest armoured Soviet tanks and tank destroyers. This, a high velocity sub-calibre tungsten-cored round, was in extremely short supply.

The 75mm KwK 42 could penetrate any frontal surface of the British Cromwell up to 2500m (8202ft) and the Churchill up to 1700m (5577ft) while remaining invulnerable to their weaponry. It was similarly effective against the American Sherman, although the Sherman's glacis plate could only be penetrated by the Panther at 100m (328ft) while the Panther remained invulnerable to its 75mm M3 gun. If faced by a Sherman mounting a heavier 76mm M1A1 gun, or a British Sherman Firefly, the Allied tanks at least stood a chance. The 76mm gun could penetrate the Panther's turret at 700m (2296ft). In frontal attack, these 7.71kg (17lb) shells could defeat the gun mantlet and turret armour, but not the hull armour of the Panther at normal combat ranges. The Panther carried 79 rounds of ammunition for the KwK 42 on the Ausf D and A and 82 rounds on the Ausf G, the redesigned hull increasing its stowage space. The recommended ratio was 50 per cent Pzgr 39/42 anti-tank shells, and 50 per cent Sprgr 42 high explosive shells. Three rounds were stowed under the turret turntable, 40 rounds were stored horizontally in pan-

niers along the superstructure sides of the hull, and 36 rounds were stored vertically in bins along the hull side. The extra three rounds for the Ausf G were amongst those in the panniers on the superstructure side.

SECONDARY AND ANCILLARY ARMAMENT

The coaxial and hull machine guns (and anti-aircraft machine gun, if installed) were a version of the superlative Rheinmetall MG 34 general purpose 7.92mm machine gun. This air-cooled weapon, designed during the early 1930s, operated on the principle of recoil assisted by muzzle blast, and used a method of locking the bolt designed by Mauser. It had an astounding rate of fire of 800–900rpm. It was like much German equipment, complicated and difficult and expensive to manufacture but nonetheless, it was an excellent machine gun, easily the best of its generation. To quote one small-arms expert: 'Actually using it was rather like using a Rolls Royce car for ploughing a field – it was too good for the task.' The version fitted to the Panther was MG 34m, specially adapted for armoured vehicles by the fitting of a thick armoured barrel. The secondary armament was provided with 4104 rounds on the Ausf D and 4200 rounds on the Ausf A and G. These were stored in bags each containing a link belt holding 150 rounds.

The early Ausf D Panthers also mounted six *Nebelwurfgerät* (smoke candle dischargers), three on each side of the turret. This practice ceased in June 1943 after a reported incident in February 1943, when enemy small-arms fire had set off the candles, incapacitating the crew. As mentioned above, the pistol ports on the turret were deleted once the provision of the *Nahverteidigungswaffe* close defence weapon system began in December 1943. This was mounted on the right hand rear of the turret roof. The 26mm grenade projector could fire smoke, signal flares and anti-personnel grenades and was traversable through 360 degrees, although its elevation was fixed at 50 degrees. Shortages meant that its deployment on Panther tanks was never total. The crew themselves had access to a single 9mm MP 40 machine pistol and each carried 9mm P38 or, more rarely, P08 automatic pistols as side arms.

Left: German paratroopers wave as they use a Panther as a means of getting into battle quickly during the Ardennes campaign in 1944. The men give a clear indication of the sheer size of a Panther.

CHAPTER 3

Production of the Panther

The Panther was evidently a superlative weapon. Designed as a direct response to the T-34, it suffered in comparison with its Soviet rival in one vital factor: ease of production. The technical brilliance of the Panther had its price: it slowed production, and its complexity resulted in numerous automotive failures on production models, causing maintenance difficulties in the field. However, extraordinary efforts were made to increase output and provide the troops with adequate numbers of the new tank.

Indeed, during 1944, despite Allied bombing, more Panthers than ever were built. Nonetheless, the Soviets still outproduced the Germans almost threefold in the vital area of medium tanks, and this quite apart from the British and Americans. The Panther was an attempt to find a qualitative solution to the problem of defeating the huge Allied tank armies, but ironically there just were not enough German tanks to stem the tide. As one German writer rather sourly noted: 'The Panther stopped the T-34 menace on the Eastern Front, the Tiger I and II could have eliminated it. They were not outfought, just outproduced.' That, however, is the point. The Panther was indeed outproduced and, in reality, 'the T-34 menace' was not stopped, because it was the T-34 which led the advance on Berlin.

THE ENIGMA OF THE GERMAN WAR ECONOMY

Germany was the economic powerhouse of the Axis, the only country which could approach the Soviet and American output. By the time the Panther entered production in late 1942, Germany, in addition to her own sizeable industrial base, had access to the resources and manufacturing facilities of occupied Europe. Yet the Allies were producing three times as many aircraft and tanks. There is no doubt that,

Left: Panther Ausf Ds outside the factory, with their gun muzzles covered. Although over 5500 Panthers were built, too few were produced to alter the course of the war.

Above: Railway flatbeds were used to transport Panthers to and from the front. Using rail saved the tanks' engines, gearboxes and moving parts, and supposedly ensured longer service in the field.

throughout the war, the Germans produced far less than its resources in materials, manpower, technical and scientific skill, and manufacturing capacity would permit. Up to 1943, Britain outproduced Germany and her European empire in almost all major weapon systems, despite Britain's far smaller economy. The Soviet Union which, due to German success was temporarily reduced to an economic base even smaller than Britain's, produced half as much again as Germany between 1942 and 1945. As historian Richard Overy notes: 'However much the statistics may mask differences in policy and circumstances, this is still a significant contrast. Had the situation been otherwise, German fighting power might well have avoided the remorseless attrition which set in in 1944.'

Moreover, the German economy had been the one most prepared for war. By the summer of 1941, considerably more than half of the German workforce was involved in military production. It was a level of commitment higher than Britain in 1941 and higher than the United States throughout the war. Germany also had access to the resources of Belgium, France, Luxembourg and Norway, almost the entire European coal and steel industry, other important mineral resources, large numbers of workers, and the manufacturing machinery and reserves of these countries. Yet German industrial output remained stable. Armament output in 1941 was little more than it had been in 1939. The reasons for this failure to increase production are complex and unclear. Certainly German bureaucracy did not help. Hitler had concentrated power in his hands to enable him to order the weapons he thought necessary, but without a centrally planned economy

like Russia's, his proposals were haphazardly implemented. To quote Overy again:

'There was no straight line of command between Führer and factory. In between lay a web of ministries, plenipotentiaries and Party commissars, each with their own apparatus, interests and rubber stamps, producing more than the usual weight of bureaucratic inertia. At the end of the line was a business community, most of whom remained wedded to entrepreneurial independence, and resented the jumbled administration, the corrupt Nazi Party hacks, the endless form-filling, which stifled what voluntary efforts they might have made to transform the war economy.'

The Germans also struggled with mass production. Their armed forces preferred working with smaller firms and skilled craftsmen, sensitive to frequent design changes and producing sophisticated specialised weapons. Their industrial economy had always been good for high quality, skilled workmanship and technical advances, all demanding time and material. Technical sophistication was routinely preferred to quantity. The Panther is a case in point. The layout of the MNH (*Maschinenfabrik Niedersachsen Hannover*) plant in Hannover resolutely ignored the mass production methods pioneered in the United States. The tanks were not built on a Ford-style production line as preferred in the West and in the Soviet Union, where each worker was assigned a limited, repetitive task. At Hannover, the Panthers were moved from station to station along the assembly line and at each station, a specific task was performed. It ensured high quality workmanship but did little to speed production.

ALBERT SPEER AND THE INCREASE IN PRODUCTION

Hitler recognised the problem and berated the military and industrial leadership for their unnecessarily complex demands. He wanted 'more primitive, robust construction' and the introduction of 'crude mass production'. However, it took his appointment of Albert Speer as minister of armaments to bring Germany to something approaching its potential. Speer established a central planning board and rationalised armament production. He closed down small firms, redistributed skilled labour, and decided the allocation and distribution of raw materials and machinery on a national level. He set up a system of committees for major weapons which were responsible for all the firms producing a particular weapon type. These committees planned and supervised all military production, resulting in large improvements in efficiency, coordination and central control.

Perhaps most importantly, he managed to reduce the role of the military in the war economy and limit their interference in production. The military had been largely responsible for constraining Germany's output of armaments. Military priorities dominated design, development and manufacturing. Factories were forced to respond to countless demands for changes in design and specification. The military also set production schedules, although they rarely consulted the industrialists and engineers. While this produced some excellent weapons, the constant tinkering and design changes slowed production. Hitler noted that his industrialists 'were always complaining about this niggardly procedure – today an order for ten howitzers, tomorrow for two mortars and so on'. This was a fairly accurate assessment of the problem. Engineers from Rechlin complained in 1944, 'Nobody would seriously believe that so much inadequacy, bungling, confusion, misplaced power, failure to recognise the truth and deviation from the reasonable really exists.' Speer brought in industrialist engineers so that production could be run by those who knew something about it. This paid considerable dividends, and output trebled over the next two years. Only the Allied bombing campaigns brought about a decline, and later collapse, of German industry. The production of the Panther illustrates the difficulties and also successes of German industry over these years.

INITIAL PRODUCTION OF THE PANTHER

MAN received confirmation that their VK 3002 design for the Panther had been chosen by Hitler and the Panzerkommission on 15 May 1942. The company soon received contracts to produce the first two experimental Panther models by August/September 1942 and begin wholesale production in the autumn. The original production programme called for 250 vehicles per month. In September 1942, this was revised, increasing output to 600 per month up to, and including, the

spring of 1944. It was clear that this programme would require the participation of other firms. The four firms selected to produce the Panther were MAN, Daimler-Benz, Henschel and MNH. MAN and Daimler-Benz were already ready to begin building in late 1942, and Henschel and MNH hoped to begin delivery in July 1943. Such a large-scale project involved numerous smaller firms: for example, Dortmund-Hörder Hüttenverein of Dortmund, Eisenwerke Oberdonau of Linz, Ruhrstahl of Hanttingen, Böhler of Kaplenberg, Bismarckhütte of Upper Silesia, Harkort-Eiken of Hagen were all involved in producing the turret and armour. Numerous other component suppliers were also used.

MAN completed the first experimental Panthers, the FGST.NR.V1, an experimental chassis, and the FGST.NR.V2, a complete tank and turret, on time. These performed satisfactorily in automotive trials in the autumn of 1942. However, MAN soon fell behind on the delivery of the first production model Panther Ausf D. The first Panther was scheduled to roll off the line of MAN's Nuremberg plant in November 1942, but production only began in that month. MAN received their first 7.5cm KwK42 gun from Rheinmetall-Borsig on 15 December 1942 and Leitz SZF1 gunsight production began on 21 December of that year. The first and second Panther Ausf Ds were finally delivered on 24 January 1943 to the test ground at Grafenwöhr. It was clear that the hurried production had resulted in severe automotive transmission and suspension problems. Indeed, the first production batch were,

Below: Panthers being unloaded. The railheads at the battle of Kursk in 1943 were some distance from the battle, and many of the early Panthers suffered mechanical breakdown on the way to the front.

SdKfz 173 Jadgpanther

2.72m (8ft 11in)

3.28m (10ft 9in)

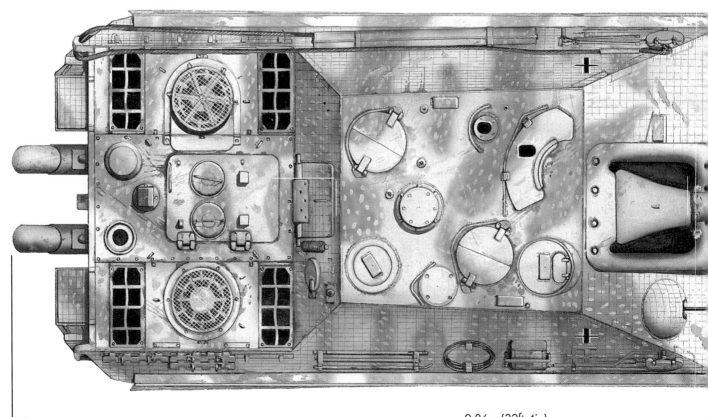

9.86m (32ft 4in)

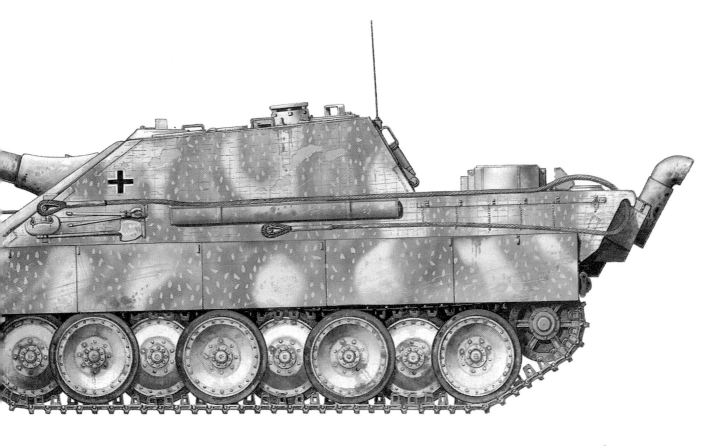

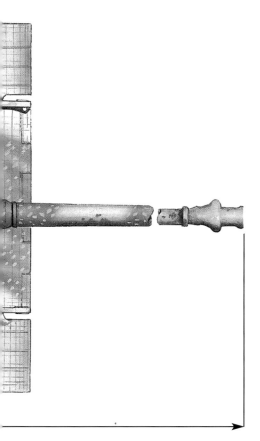

PANTHER PRODUCTION

Ausf D

Month	MAN	D-B	Henschel	MNH
Jan 43	4	0	-	-
Feb 43	11	6	0	1
Mar 43	25	14	10	19
Apr 43	0	19	26	39
May 43	68	60	25	41
Jun 43	31	40	25	36
Jul 43	58	65	19	48
Aug 43	38	26	15	36
Sep 43	7	20	10	-
Total:	242	250	130	220
Total production:				**842**

Ausf A

Month	MAN	D-B	MNH	Demag
Aug 43	-	-	3	0
Sep 43	46	50	45	(8)
Oct 43	104	90	50	(13)
Nov 43	76	71	75	(10)
Dec 43	114	82	60	(11)
Jan 44	105	90	75	(8)
Feb 44	106	70	90	-
Mar 44	94	85	90	-
Apr 44	-	105	100	-
May 44	-	32	111	-
Jun 44	-	-	120	-
Jul 44	-	-	11	-
Total:	645	675	830	50
Total production:				**2200**

NOTE: Demag totals are estimates based on the consolidated production from the Waffenamt. The Demag records were lost during the war.

Ausf G

Month	MAN	D-B	MNH
Mar 44	2	-	-
Apr 44	105	-	-
May 44	125	78	-
Jun 44	130	120	-
Jul 44	135	125	108
Aug 44	155	70	131
Sep 44	140	80	120
Oct 44	78	100	96
Nov 44	103	115	100
Dec 44	100	105	80
Jan 45	20	109	80
Feb 45	22	41	65
Mar 45	8	32	26
Apr 45	20	29	-
Total:	1143	1004	806
Total production:			**2953**

Source: Thomas L. Jentz, Germany's Panther Tank, Atglen, PA: Schiffer, 1995

to quote German armoured expert F.M. von Senger und Etterlin, 'almost without exception, unfit for front line service'. The first 60 or so Panthers built before April 1943 had to be withdrawn from service and rebuilt. This programme consisted of large-scale modifications to the motor compartment, steering gear, final drives, brakes, suspension and transmission. The turret also required considerable adaption.

Despite the early Panthers' mechanical problems and poor performance at the battle of Kursk, it was clear that it was an excellent tank. Demands for the Panther increased and it was given an SS priority rating. However, the firms building the tank were struggling to even get near the production totals demanded. Hauptdienstleiter Saur from Speer's Ministry of Armament visited MAN because Hitler, anxious to know the progress of the production of the new tank, wanted reliable information. The manufacturers could not meet the target set for Panther production for May 1943. Instead of the 308 Panthers ordered, or even the earlier figure of 250, Saur had to report to the Führer that the best that could be done was 100: 40 from MAN, 30 from Daimler-Benz, 20 from Henschel, and 10 from MNH. The situation was not helped by a further batch of Panthers, produced that month, suffering from serious mechanical failures. Once again, a massive rebuild programme had to be instituted in June 1943. On top of all this, numerous difficulties occurred on the Maybach HL 230 P30 engine, and the rebuild programme ran into February 1944.

Production of the Ausf D ran from January to September 1943, in which time 850 tanks were produced, although many of them needed extensive rebuilds. The improved Ausf A entered production at MNH in August 1943, and MAN, Daimler-Benz, and Demag of Benrath began production a month later. Henschel was diverted to the production of the Bergepanther Ausf A. The major difference between the Ausf D and A was a new, improved turret. However, problems with the Maybach HL 230 P30 engine led to modifications during the production line, starting in September 1943. The Ausf A production line ran until May 1944, during which 2100 vehicles were produced. The final model to enter production was the Ausf G. In an effort to ease production, the whole design was simplified and the slant of the upper side of the hull was reduced from 40 degrees to 30. In order to maintain the equivalent protection, however, the thickness of the armour plate had to be increased from 40mm (1.57in) to 50mm (1.96in). The Ausf G was created solely by redesigning the chassis; the turret remained exactly the same as that of the Ausf A. The transition from Ausf A to Ausf G was staggered at two-month intervals across the assembly firms MAN, Daimler-Benz and MNH. Production started at MAN in March 1944, and 3126 Ausf Gs were produced between then and April 1945, when the Allied armies overran the plants.

DISRUPTION CAUSED BY ALLIED BOMBING

Production at Daimler-Benz Werk 40 and MAN was seriously disrupted by bombing raids in August 1943. However pro-

Above: A camouflaged column of Panthers waiting to be moved by rail. By 1943–4 railways were a favourite target of Allied fighter-bombers, which severely disrupted German armour movement.

duction ran fairly smoothly until the summer of 1944, and the assembly firms began to meet their deadlines. During that summer, Allied bombing by the RAF at night, and the USAAF by day, began to take its toll. Daimler-Benz was attacked on 6 August, and again by the RAF on the night of 23/24 August 1944. The MAN plant at Nuremberg was raided on 10 September, 3 and 19 October 1944. Just as the factory had completed its repairs, it was hit on 3 January 1945 during a raid by 521 RAF bombers, causing serious damage. This was followed by two heavy American daylight raids between 20–22 February 1945. The MNH plant in Hannover was only attacked late in the war, on 14 and 28 March 1945.

The effects of Allied bombing were twofold. There was the direct effect of halting or disrupting production, reducing the number of tanks built. Both American daylight precision bombing and RAF nighttime bombing also had an effect on the city containing the factory. Water, gas and electricity supplies were disrupted, railway lines cut, roads blocked and smaller component-producing factories hit. Admittedly, much of the damage could be repaired fairly quickly and production resumed within days, weeks or possibly months. However, bombing also produced endless indirect problems, interrupting work and demoralising the workers. The population became anxious, tired and listless. As one civilian said, 'One can't get used to the raids. I wished for an end. We all got nerves. We did not get enough sleep and were very tense.' At the Ford plant in the Ruhr, which suffered some of the heaviest bombing, absenteeism was 25 per cent of the workforce during 1944. At the BMW works in Munich, which suffered far less, the rates were 20 per cent of the workforce in the summer of 1944. Similar figures can be applied to the

factories building Panthers, seriously disrupting production. Bombing also disrupted mass production. G. von Heydekampf, Speer's deputy responsible for tank production, explained after the war that the bombing forced him to modify production methods by 'the breaking down and dispersal of plants, starting up factories on account of their geographical position instead of their technical capacity...' German production facilities were often forced to disperse into smaller, better hidden premises in the country or even underground, making it extremely difficult to expand production. In January 1945, Albert Speer and his colleagues estimated that in 1944 Germany had produced 35 per cent less tanks than planned due to Allied bombing.

Although Germany had managed to increase tank production in 1944, the German Army was still being equipped with a bewildering array of armoured vehicles, and at one point the army was equipped with 151 different makes of lorry and 150 different motorcycles. Much of this was down to Hitler. He might demand German industry adopt Soviet methods of production, but this did not stop him from diverting design and production facilities on to useless projects, such as the huge Maus tank. Such projects diverted vital resources from the essential need to produce more Panthers. To quote tank expert Richard Ogorkiewicz, 'In fact, the failure to concentrate on one or two satisfactory designs like the Russians did with their T-34 was the Germans' greatest failing and a major lesson of their tank development.'

CHAPTER 4

Combat Performance: World War II Eastern Front, 1943–5

The Panzer V (Panther) was undoubtedly an excellent main battle tank and as such it formed the basis for much post-1945 tank design. It combined a formidable mix of firepower, armour and mobility, outclassing most of its opponents, such as the Sherman and the T-34/76. Even compared to the later Allied tanks – such as the M-26 Pershing, upgunned Sherman, and the T-34/85 – the Panther's high-velocity gun was able to engage at longer ranges and so dominate the battlefield.

On the open steppes of the Eastern Front, and in the fight for France and Germany in 1944–5, the Panther repeatedly proved itself against the huge Allied tank armies advancing on Germany. Its 75mm (2.95in) L/70 gun had tremendous hitting power, while its steeply sloping front armour gave it defensive strength in any head-on encounter. Most armour experts agree that the Panther was the best tank of World War II, but with two notable reservations: firstly, the mechanical performance of the Panther was poor and this lack of mechanical stamina marred the Panther's record; secondly, as has been seen, German industrial production was not capable of turning out the Panther in sufficient numbers from the factories to alter the course of the war. Allied strategic bombing, coupled with the Germans' obsession with producing quality weapons over quantity, added to the low production figures. As well as being marred by engine failure and shortage in numbers, the Panther's active service career was short: it entered service in July 1943 and finished its war in

Left: A well battened-down Panther gives covering fire on the Eastern Front. When working in tandem with panzergrenadiers, the Panther proved an excellent close-support weapon.

Above: By 1944 the Germans were very short of oil, as the Allies bombed the Ploesti oilfields in Romania. This severely hampered the Panther's freedom of action on the battlefield.

May 1945. During this period, it was on the Eastern Front that the Panther first saw service and fought its longest and toughest war.

OPERATION BARBAROSSA AND THE T-34/76, JUNE 1941

The development of the Panther was a direct response to the T-34/76 which the Soviets had deployed following the German invasion of the Soviet Union in 1941. In the largely obsolescent Soviet tank force in 1941, there were some 1000 T-34/76 tanks and they proved themselves to be quite differ-

ent opposition for the German Panzers advancing east. Armed with a powerful, long 76.2mm gun, the T-34 could hold off the German Panzers; its mathematically angled hull armour, which overhung the tracks, gave ballistic protection twice that of the 45mm (1.77in) armour used, and the sloped armour was vital for defence. In addition, the high performance diesel engine and wide tracks gave the T-34 a mobility to match that of the German Panzers.

The T-34 was a remarkable tank and required a German response. In one early battle, one T-34 shrugged off 24 37mm armour-piercing rounds from German anti-tank guns, only retiring from the field of battle when a subsequent round slammed into its turret and caused it to jam. The problem for the Soviet High Command was that there were too few T-34s and too many older T-26s, T-28s and BTs which were quickly being destroyed by the Germans.

In his book *Panzer Leader*, the German tank general Heinz Guderian described the shock felt by the Germans on first coming across the T-34 in 1941: 'Numerous Russian T-34s went into action and inflicted heavy losses on the German tanks at Mzensk in 1941. Up to this time, we had enjoyed tank superiority, but from now on the situation was reversed. The prospect of rapid decisive victories was fading in consequence. I made a report on the situation ... and sent it to the Army Group. In this report I described in plain terms the marked superiority of the T-34 to our PzKpfw IV and drew the relevant conclusion as that must affect our future tank production.' Until the earliest encounters with the T-34, there had been no plans to change the German tank building programme with the Panzer IV. A heavier 30.5-tonne (30-ton) tank had been ordered as far back as 1937, and an even heavier 66.04-tonne (65-ton) tank a year later, but production of both had been put on hold. The Panzer III and, more especially, the Panzer IV, had proved themselves in the campaigns in Poland in 1939, the Low Countries and France in 1940, and then the Balkans and Greece in 1941, and so there seemed no need for Germany to alter a tried and tested Panzer arsenal which had succeeded in so many previous campaigns. However, after meeting the T-34, the Germans looked seriously at building a heavier tank to counter it and pulled the 1930s 30.5-tonne (30-ton) prototype plan out of mothballs.

UPGRADING GERMAN ARMOUR

Following inspections of captured T-34s, the Germans instituted various stop-gap measures. They re-equipped the Panzer Mark III with the 50mm (1.96in) L60 main gun. This was, however, only a temporary expedient considering the poor performance overall of the Mark III compared with the T-34. The Germans also took their main battle tank, the Panzer IV, and fitted it with the long-barrelled 75mm gun which achieved sufficiently high muzzle velocity to take on the T-34. With various modifications, the Mark IV provided the German army with its tank 'workhorse' for the entire war. Simultaneously, however, the Germans also pushed on with the design for heavier tanks to match the Soviet T-34 and heavier KV series tanks. This came to fruition with the Panther, Tiger and King Tiger tanks, all of which were specifically built to fight successful tank actions with Allied tanks such as the T-34, a number of whose features, such as sloped and angled armour, were incorporated into the Panther. However, as the Germans were loath to accept the superiority of the T-34 – built, after all, by a racially inferior people, according to Nazi ideology – they went their own way with tank design. The fact that the Germans also had problems in copying the T-34's aluminium engine added to the impetus to produce an 'all-German' tank design for their new Panzer V 'Panther' tank.

Above: An SS tank crew private from the *Liebstandarte* Division wearing a two-piece drill uniform issued in 1944. His pink shoulder straps indicate he is a member of the panzer arm.

THE PANTHER AND PREPARATIONS
FOR THE BATTLE OF KURSK, 1943

First completed by late 1942, the Panther received its baptism of fire during 'Operation Citadel' (or 'Zitadelle') in the summer of 1943. Citadel was the German summer offensive against a Soviet bulge in the lines around the town of Kursk, an important rail junction some 805km (500 miles) to the south of Moscow. The 1942–3 winter campaign had left a bulge 190km (118 miles) wide and 120.7km (75 miles) deep in the front around the city. The battle of Kursk called for converging attacks by two German armies against the northern and southern flanks of the Soviet bulge, with the aim of nipping out the salient, capturing or destroying the Soviet forces involved, and using the victory as a springboard for future attacks. To fight this battle, the German Army would need to employ the bulk of the Panzer armies so painstakingly built up following the defeat at the battle of Stalingrad.

In February 1943, Guderian had been brought in to take over the Eastern Front. Reinstated as Inspector General of Armoured Troops, Guderian aimed to build fully equipped tank divisions, rather than a number of partially equipped ones. He wanted divisions capable of large-scale operations, each equipped with 400 tanks and a balanced mix of supporting arms, by 1944. Far better, he urged, to have only a few hard-hitting divisions than many weak ones. He believed that

Germany should ultimately have large Panzer armies capable of taking on the Soviet tank armies which were being equipped from factories east of the Ural mountains.

Guderian looked at the war in the round with a view to a prolonged war. He stressed the need to improve the Panther's reliability and also wanted to make sure that while Panther and Tiger production increased, it was not at the

Below: Panthers in formation advancing across the Russian steppe. In combat they would disperse into a fighting formation. These are Panther Ausf As, the second production variant.

expense of the Panzer IV, the well-tried workhorse of the German Army. Therefore, he was not keen on the whole Kursk operation, preferring to wait for an attack in 1944. However, Hitler ignored Guderian's concerns about the irreplaceable losses in men and tanks an offensive in 1943 would cause, and authorised Operation Citadel. Hitler then interfered further by insisting that the operation required

Above: The Panther commander's view of battle. In combat the hatch was usually closed, but many commanders preferred to risk remaining exposed in order to have a better idea of the battle's progress.

more Panthers, leading to delays in the attack's starting date. Hitler's decision was the worst of both worlds and compounded the German situation. By July 1943, the month Kursk would be launched, the Germans' delay cost them the element of surprise, and they were forced to attack over fortified ground of the enemy's choosing and on which there was little room to manoeuvre. Meanwhile, the delay had not been long enough for sufficient numbers of heavy tanks like the Panther to arrive at the front and, as will be seen, nor did it allow its manufacturers sufficient time to sort out mechanical teething difficulties. Those which did arrive at the front were often unfit for service.

The battle of Kursk was certainly unique. It was the greatest tank battle in history, involving over 6000 tanks and self-propelled guns. By contrast, the battle of El Alamein in North

Africa in 1942 involved around 1500 tanks; later battles such as the battle of 'Chinese Farm' in the 1973 Arab–Israeli War in the Sinai saw some 2000 tanks deployed. Kursk is seen as the swansong of the German armoured forces, yet it is ironic to note that the German Army undertook its last great armoured offensive in the east with an armoured force that was largely obsolescent. Although some 900,000 Germans with 2700 fighting vehicles assembled for the battle of Kursk, of those 2700 vehicles employed by the Germans in the attack, only a relatively small number were Panthers, and an even smaller proportion were Tigers; the majority of German tanks at Kursk were Panzer IVs armed with the long 75mm gun. Once again, insufficient thought given to numbers and stress on quality meant the Germans lacked sufficient Panthers. This would be part of the reason that the German attack was defeated.

The Panther was simply not ready for action at Kursk. The roads and tracks between the railheads and the assembly areas for Kursk were soon littered with Panthers which had broken down with transmission failures and engine fires. As has been seen, Guderian was well aware that Hitler was rushing the Panthers into action too early, and before they had been fully tested on the training grounds. Guderian's appraisal was that 'the Panthers, on whose performance the Chief of the Army General Staff was relying so heavily, were still suffering from many teething troubles inherent in all new equipment and it seemed unlikely that these could all be put right in time for the launching of the attack'.

Guderian was right. The delay caused by Hitler's obsession with controlling operations gave the Soviets added time to transform the Kursk salient into an impregnable fortress, and this they did with speed and completeness. They constructed six interlocking defensive belts to a depth of 40.23km (25 miles) with covering belts of trenches, strongpoints and barbed wire. Supporting these defences in depth were 20,000 guns, of which one-third were anti-tank weapons. Simultaneously, the Russians laid minefields to a density of 2500 anti-personnel and 2200 anti-tank mines per mile of front. In all, 400,000 mines were laid; streams were dammed to make impassable flooded areas, and otherwise rich, fertile farmland was turned into a gigantic obstacle course for the attacking Germans. The Soviet High Command (or Stavka) pressed local Russian civilians into digging 4828km (3000 miles) of defensive trenches, carefully criss-crossed to allow mobility for the Russian infantry. Artillery, anti-tank and machine gun nests were sited to provide mutual support and create a 'curtain of fire' with which to meet the German attack.

Backing up these defences, the Russians amassed a huge force of fighters and bombers, and the biggest tank force ever. Into the bulge at Kursk, the Russians crammed seven armies. Meanwhile, reserve forces of a tank army and two infantry armies were concentrated 241km (150 miles) behind the front. The reserve armies built additional defen-

Above: The Panther gave the Germans the ability to match the Soviet T-34s in terms of equipment, but the superior training of the German crews gave them an advantage in combat.

sive belts in front of their positions. When all the preparations were complete, 1,336,000 men, 3444 tanks, 2900 aircraft and 19,000 guns were ready for the battle of Kursk. Seventy-five per cent of all Russian armour was now located in and around Kursk, waiting to strike a hammer blow.

THE BATTLE OF KURSK

The Germans knew that the Russians were fortifying the Kursk salient yet, under Hitler's direction, still went ahead with their attack. As mentioned earlier, the delays to the attack at Kursk favoured the Soviets, giving them time to prepare while not allowing time for sufficient Panthers to arrive at the front. In the end, the Germans deployed just two Panther-equipped tank battalions to participate in Kursk, and these fought on the southern front in a separate 'Battle Group Kempf'. In addition, the Germans reinforced some of their Panzer divisions with a third tank battalion with the formidable Tiger tank. The other two battalions used a variety of tanks. Most Panzer divisions at Kursk had battalions equipped with the Panzer III and IV. However, one or two divisions, such as the 11th Panzer, besides a battalion of Tigers, also had a battalion of Panzer IVs and one of Panthers.

Thus Panthers fought in penny packets in units other than the 'Kempf' battle group.

On 5 July 1943, Hermann Hoth's Fourth Panzer Army of 18 divisions (10 armoured) attacked from the south of Kursk, while simultaneously Walther Model's Ninth Army, also of 18 divisions (7 armoured) attacked in the north. In all, some 250 Panther Ausf D tanks participated in Operation Citadel, mostly in the 51st and 52nd Panzer Battalions which were combined into the improvised 'Kempf' Panther Brigade. At Kursk, the Panther Ausf D made an inauspicious operational debut on 5 July, as these tanks suffered severe reliability problems in combat due to frequent mechanical breakdowns. Many had difficulties even reaching the front line, as has been seen in the preparations for Kursk, when many Panthers suffered engine fires caused by insufficient levels of engine cooling and ventilation. This problem resulted from the watertight sealing of the engine compartment to prepare the tank for amphibious wading. In addition, there was widespread damage to gears, transmission, and suspension. All these prevented the Panther from living up to German expectations. Moreover, operationally, the dense Soviet minefields outlined above were not properly cleared and so inflicted a heavy toll on the Panthers. This combination of mechanical and tactical problems resulted in the 51st Panzer Battalion suffering a disastrous 56 per cent loss rate on its first day of action. By the second day of the Kursk offensive, just one-fifth of the

Above: A Panther Ausf D captured at Kursk in 1943 on display in Moscow, being eagerly examined by Red Army soldiers. The Panther was rushed into the battle before it was fully ready for combat.

Panthers committed remained operational, a tremendous drop-out rate testifying to the ill-judged speed with which the tanks were thrown into combat.

Gefreiter Werner Kriegel in a Panther of the 51st Panzer Battalion recalled the bitter fighting at Kursk: 'Our first attack stuck in a minefield. I lost a track. While our artillery suppressed the Soviets, we could recover both disabled tanks ... the first day ended in disaster. By the evening of the 5th, Panzer Battalion 51 had only 22 Panthers operational. Some 28 tanks or so were totally destroyed, the rest damaged. My comrades complained of weak final drives and of their engines overheating ... On the 8 July we again headed for Obojan south of Kursk. Our Panther received a hit from a tank gun on the commander's cupola. We carried on the attack with an open hatch and a cracked cupola. My commander still has the shell ... We lost one tank to one of these heavy assault guns [SU-152], the mantlet was simply penetrated. We also met American tanks [supplied to the Soviets under Lend-Lease], which were no match for us ... We destroyed a number of T-34s at ranges well over 2500 metres.'

Kriegel's Panthers fought on the southern edge of the Kursk salient as a separate detachment to Hoth's Fourth Panzer Army which spearheaded the main attack. With nine Panzer divisions, including the cream of the SS Panzer units (Leibstandarte, Das Reich and Totenkopf), the Germans managed an advance of almost 32km (20 miles). The Germans made their farthest advance in the south when elements of the Leibstandarte established a bridgehead over the small Psel river. Hoth then swung the weight of his attack towards the minor rail junction at the town of Prokhorovka. This led to a decisive and remarkable armoured engagement when massed Russian armour fought the Germans to a standstill.

THE BATTLE OF PROKHOROVKA

For the push on Prokhorovka, Hoth had more than 500 tanks, including those Panthers which had not broken down or been destroyed. To overcome the superior Tigers and Panthers, the T-34s were told to engage the Germans at such close range that their guns would be able to knock out the tanks. This was the armoured equivalent of hand-to-hand combat. The aim was to use the T-34's superior manoeuvrability to get behind and to the side of the Germans to exploit the weaker side and rear armour of their heavier tanks.

On the morning of 12 July, two armies faced one another at the town of Prokhorovka. Some 850 Soviet tanks against 600 German tanks would fight the largest tank engagement of the war. At 0830 hours, Pavel Rotmistrov, the Soviet commander, gave the codeword to attack: 'Steel, steel', (in Russian

Above: A three-quarter view of a Panther Ausf D, with a number of features clearly visible, including the smoke launchers on the side of the turret, the shrouded headlights and the viewing periscopes.

Stalin). The T-34s rolled forward over a 4.82km (3 miles) front into a head-on collision. Waves of T-34s suddenly appeared at speed, attacking obliquely to the German line. This ran against all the rules of the tactical manuals for armoured warfare and deprived the few Panthers the luxury

of picking off their opponents at a great distance using their powerful main armament.

As the Russian official history recalled, the closeness of the engagement disadvantaged the Germans: 'It destroyed the enemy's ability to control his leading units and subunits. The close combat deprived the Tigers of the advantages which their powerful gun and thick armour conferred, and they were successfully shot up at close range by the T-34s. Immense numbers of tanks were mixed up all over the bat-

support. The T-34s rolled up to point blank range where their guns ripped into the sides and rears of the Panthers and Tigers. When the T-34s ran out of ammunition they were rammed into the German tanks; dismounted T-34 crews on foot then set about destroying German tanks.

By the end of the day – one never likely to be repeated in the history of armoured warfare – 700 tanks lay battered and broken on the battlefield. With hulls pierced and turrets ripped off, the scene was remarkable. While thousands of charred or burning corpses littered this grotesque landscape, the Russians had won and the German attack had been decisively blunted and no breakthrough achieved. The victory owed much to the T-34 tank, but also decisive in victory was the determination of the Russian tank crews to take on the Germans at close range.

After Kursk, German hopes for a victory in 1943 evaporated; after Kursk, the Germans would never launch a major offensive again, and the Russians began their inexorable advance to Berlin. The German armoured divisions which had borne the brunt of much of the fighting were devastated. Some Panzer divisions were down to 17 tanks. In total, the Fourth Panzer Army lost around 300 tanks at the battle of Prokhorovka, including the remaining Panthers. While Soviet losses had totalled some 400 tanks, Russian industrial capacity was such that these losses would quickly be replaced. Also, as the Russians had been left in control of the battlefield at Kursk, they were able to salvage their lightly damaged tanks, and as they fought Kursk with only one type of tank, the T-34, spares problems were simplified. By contrast, the Germans fought Kursk with five separate tanks and two assault guns which made repairs that much more complicated as each model needed specific spares.

THE PANTHER AT KURSK

The Panther, while a potential war winner, failed to turn the battle of Kursk. The combat experience of the Panther at Kursk was problematic. While the Panthers were capable of knocking out T-34s at great ranges, the paucity of Panthers and their propensity to break down diminished their importance. The Panther had been built too quickly, without time for thorough tests and evaluations. As a consequence, the Panther suffered problems with the drive system for the tank well into 1944. As has been seen, the cramped and sealed engine unit overheated the engine and caused fires. Engine fires in the middle of combat were not uncommon, adding to the strains of the Panther crew. One Panther crew member recalled an incident in September 1944 when his unit was passing through a pine forest: 'The vibrations of the heavy tanks resulted in a steady rain of pine needles. After a short time, the first tank broke down, and others followed. We examined the incident. The pine needles had fallen into the air inlets and blocked it. The respective engines had stopped almost immediately. As a stop-gap solution we welded a perforated bucket over the rear air inlet.'

tlefield; there was neither time nor space to disengage and re-form ranks. Fired at short range, shells penetrated front and side armour. There were frequent explosions as ammunition blew up, throwing tank turrets dozens of yards from their stricken vehicles ... On the scorched black earth, smashed tanks were blazing like torches. It was difficult to tell who was attacking and who was defending.' Smoke and dusk soon obscured the fighting, and the tanks became so interlocked that it was impossible to call up artillery or air

Above: Panzergrenadiers advance alongside a Panther through a wheatfield on the Eastern Front. The *Schürzen* or side skirts were introduced to give greater protection against Soviet anti-tank rifles.

SOVIET TACTICS: PAKFRONTS

The Panthers on the Eastern Front were up against a more formidable foe than the one encountered in 1941 in the drive on Moscow. The Red Army which fought the Germans at Kursk – and afterwards in the drive to Berlin – was quite different from the brave but badly trained and poorly co-ordinated troops who had faced the Germans in 1941. Kursk showed a new level of confidence in both defence and offence. In defence, the Soviets established what the Germans called 'Pakfronts'. These were a complex pattern of strongpoints, based upon groups of tanks, anti-tank guns protected by deep minefields, and sited to a depth of over 19.3km (12 miles). These Pakfronts called for new tactics by the Germans as the Russian system meant that in battle, up to 10 guns would open up on the German lead tank.

PANTHER TACTICS: THE *PANZERKEIL* AND *PANZERGLOCKE*

The Panthers at Kursk and after were built into formations known as *Panzerkeil*. This was an armoured wedge, spearheaded by heavy tanks to force its way into the Soviet Pakfront, with medium and light tanks echeloned off on the flanks. The Panther would often find itself at the armoured

tip with the Tigers, with the more vulnerable Panzer IIIs and IVs protected by these heavier tanks. Behind the armoured wedge would come the infantry with machine guns, artillery support and command vehicles.

The *Panzerkeil* system evolved into the *Panzerglocke* by 1944. This was a bell-shaped attacking formation with armoured engineers following up the lead Panthers and Tigers. As before, lighter tanks covered the flanks. With the *Panzerglocke* there would be a command group, including the Panther variant command tank (see variants section), to control the armoured formation and supporting air strikes from Luftwaffe bombers and Ju 87 'Stuka' dive bombers. These new tactics depended upon certain criteria: adequate reconnaissance; good ground-to-air communication; high levels of tank gunnery; maintenance of momentum; correct positioning of Forward Observers; sufficient reserves of fuel and ammunition close to the attacking tip, and the correct use of white and coloured tank smoke for screening and marking on the battlefield.

MELLENTHIN'S ASSESSMENT

The German Panzer commander, Major-General F.W. von Mellenthin, left an interesting record of the Panther's performance at Kursk in his book *Panzer Battles*. It says much about the initial problems of the Panther: 'During Citadel the German armour moved and fought in wedge formation, the

Panzerkeil, which up to then had proved very effective indeed; the spearhead of the wedge was formed by the heaviest tanks, and the Tigers proved their worth against the Russian anti-tank [Pak] fronts organised in depth. The Tiger's 88-mm gun was superior to anything the Russians had, but as I have mentioned, the Panthers were still in their infancy and were a failure.' Mellenthin's comments say much about the problems of trying out a new weapon on the battlefield when it had not finished its trials on the training ground.

BATTLE OF KHARKOV, AUGUST 1943

The ability of the Germans to inflict local defeats after Kursk was proved when the Soviets went on to the offensive. After their victory at Kursk, the Soviets tried to go on to take the strategically important city of Kharkov. Stalin allotted the task to the élite Fifth Guards Tank Army. As with at Kursk, the Germans knew that the Soviets were going to attack and organised a defence in depth. Included in the Germans' defence were 96 Panthers and, when the Soviets attacked in August 1943, these Panthers badly mauled the Fifth Guards. The Soviets, fresh from their victory at Kursk, realised the danger of underestimating the Germans: some 420 tanks from one of the best Soviet tank units were destroyed. Although at Kharkov, the Germans demonstrated their tactical superiority, what they lacked was the strategical momentum to do anything other than inflict tactical defeats on the Soviets' advance inexorably west

THE PANTHER DEFENCE AT NARVA

In defence – and after Kursk, the Germans were increasingly on the defensive – the Panther could turn individual battles. During late 1943, the 11th SS Volunteer Panzergrenadier Division Nordland received some Panther tanks instead of StuG III assault guns (the normal equipment for this type of SS division). By early 1944, the Nordland formed part of SS-Gruppenführer (Lieutenant-General) Felix Steiner's III Germanic SS Panzer Corps, holding the northern part of the Eastern Front on the Gulf of Finland at Narva. The front line in the north had changed only slightly since December 1941, although the Soviets had managed to break the German encirclement of Leningrad in 1943. The Soviets launched an offensive against the Nordland's defensive line along the frozen Narva River in early February 1944, establishing a bridgehead south of the positions held by the German division. They began to advance north, rolling up the SS defences from the south. In desperation, the divisional commander committed his reserve of Panther Ausf A tanks from the 11th SS Panzer Battalion Hermann von Salza – named after the Grand Master of the Teutonic Knights – and stemmed the Soviet advance. Similarly, when in late March, a Soviet armoured column broke through the German defences and reached the main bridge over the Narva at Ivangorod, the Nordland committed the Panthers of its 1st Panzer Company to frantic counter-attacks against vastly superior Soviet

forces. For his courage in this action, SS-Oberscharführer (Sergeant) Phillip Wild received the coveted Knights Cross. The III SS Panzer Corps managed to conduct an epic defence at Narva against superior odds for six months before a massive Soviet onslaught in July 1944 forced them to withdraw.

IMPROVEMENTS TO THE PANTHER

Steady improvements to the Panther in late 1943 and early 1944 added to its potency. The inadequate letterbox machine gun was replaced by a ball mount; extra cooling pipes attached to the left exhaust kept down engine overheating. In addition, from September 1943 the Panthers were painted with an anti-magnetic Zimmerit paste. The paste was applied to all vertical surfaces on the Panther and was designed to resist the magnetic mines supposedly being used by Soviet infantry. Zimmerit was applied to all new tanks in the factory, and tanks already in service were painted in the field by the crews, but the paste had drawbacks. While it helped protect the Panthers against infantry assault, there were rumours it caused engine fires; also, it would seem that Soviet infantry were not equipped with magnetic mines in any quantity so Zimmerit was redundant anyway. It did, however, give the Panthers a distinctive appearance.

By early 1944, the Eastern Front had stabilised after a series of retreats by the Germans. The mechanical defects of the Panther were being tackled and in its defensive role, the

Below: A deadly combination of Panther and panzergrenadier armed with a flamethrower. Both weapons were useful in clearing prepared Soviet positions.

Above: With the Germans on the defensive from 1943 onwards, camouflage measures such as these became increasingly common. Here a Panther's distinctive profile has been disguised by wheat.

Panther, as at the battle at Narva, proved its worth. The accuracy and punch of the 75mm gun allowed the Panther to destroy any enemy tank at distances from 2011m (2200yds). The Panther was also deployed across the Panzer units and not in special formations like the Tiger tank. During 1944–45, the Soviets gained a very healthy respect for its combat power, and made great efforts to recover and repair disabled vehicles so that the Red Army could deploy several Panther-equipped tank companies against the vehicle's inventors.

THE PANTHER AND THE SOVIET SUMMER OFFENSIVES OF 1944

On 22 June 1944, the third anniversary of Operation Barbarossa, Soviet T-34s spearheaded a huge attack on the German lines, pushing the Germans back 724.2km (450 miles) and destroying 25 German divisions. This advance proved how much Russian armour had improved, both in their tactics and standard of equipment. The Russians now

had sufficient armour to build huge tank armies which dwarfed anything the Germans could put into the field, and the Germans were now outnumbered three-to-one. The tables were finally turning from the heady days of 1941 when the Wehrmacht had smashed into Russia and driven to the gates of Moscow.

All along the front, Soviet forces moved forward in a series of set-piece battles which took advantage of their limitless manpower and huge tank forces. Typically, after a heavy bombardment, an attack would be spearheaded by heavy tanks which would penetrate the German defences and force an opening for the following T-34s and infantry. The problem for the Germans was that there were too few Panthers available to halt the Soviets. The Soviets had the resources to attack again and again over the same ground and eventually wear down the German defenders.

Against these attacks, the Germans organised the Panthers into mobile counter-attack units. These units would slice into the flank of any Soviet attack once the attack was underway. As many Soviet tanks were without radios, the Soviets relied on their tank crews following pre-arranged tactics in which each tank was only prepared for its part in the attack. This

rigidity meant that German counter-attacks seldom met a coordinated response, and the Panthers and Panzer IVs were able to inflict much larger losses than would usually have been the case. Certainly, they were not able to use similar tactics against the better trained Allied tank crews in Italy and Normandy.

What thwarted the Germans was the sheer weight of Soviet matériel coupled to illogical 'no retreat' orders issued by Hitler. Panthers, along with countless German troops, found themselves surrounded in the battles of 1944. These encircled troops either surrendered or fought 'Cauldron' (*Kesselschlachten*) battles to break the encirclement. In such battles, casualties were high, and they placed a premium on serviceable Panthers. Panthers were therefore organised into special rescue units to relieve trapped pockets of Germans. One formation specially raised for this purpose was the Heavy Panzer Regiment Bäke, named after its commander, Oberstleutnant Franz Bäke. The regiment combined one Tiger battalion with 34 tanks, a Panther battalion with 46 tanks, and balanced supporting arms, including an infantry battalion, self-propelled artillery and engineer bridging units.

Below: The Jagdpanther, with its potent 88mm (3.46in) gun. The Jagdpanther was probably the finest tank destroyer of World War II, and even more feared than the Panther by the Allies.

In one action in January 1944, Bäke's unit fought for five days, destroying no fewer than 267 Soviet tanks for the loss of only one Tiger and four Panthers. Bäke's unit then provided the vanguard of the III Panzer Corps as it drove to the relief of trapped German troops who were attempting to escape Soviet encirclement. In all these engagements, the Panthers proved their worth, but they were too few in number to do any more than delay the Soviet push west.

One Soviet tank lieutenant, Degan, recalled the difficulty of fighting a tank such as the Panther: 'I couldn't do anything with a German tank like a Tiger or Panther if I met it head on. If I was going to win, I had to find its weak spot, and that meant approaching it from the side. So our usual tactics, when we were advancing and knew that there might be a tank ambush ahead, was to advance suddenly, stop and open fire as if we knew there was something there, and often turn around and take to our heels. We hoped they would open fire, and we would then be able to see where they were firing from and could then fight back.'

It was supply difficulties which halted the Russian summer 1944 offensive, rather than any real opposition. The Russians were now established in Poland and East Prussia, the heartland of German militarism, and stood poised to move into Germany itself. The remaining German Panthers fought with tenacity and courage but sheer weight of numbers overwhelmed them. When the Russian advance stabilised along the line of the Vistula river, the Germans attempted to shore up their front to meet the next Russian attack. To make matters worse for Germany, Romania, allied to Germany, fell out of the war. Russian troops of Roman Malinovsky's Second Ukrainian Front struck out to take advantage of Rumania's collapse and, spearheaded by the Sixth Tank Army, took Bucharest in September 1944. More importantly, Russia captured the Ploesti oil fields, one of Germany's last remaining sources of crude oil. Soon German Panthers would be grounded by lack of fuel.

The problem for the Panther crews was that after Kursk, the momentum of the war was towards Germany. Therefore, they were increasingly fighting in a defensive role rather than in the attacking formations described above. While it was a big improvement over the Panzer IV, Guderian was forced to count on the more reliable (and abundant) Panzer IV to the war's end, so resisted attempts to end production in favour of heavier but more temperamental tanks such as the Panther.

THE BATTLE FOR POLAND

Having advanced into Poland, the Soviet commander, Georgi Zhukov, planned the final offensive into Germany and on to Berlin. By October 1944, the plans for a new offensive were well advanced and 13 mechanised corps were established to provide the main thrust into the Reich. These corps were made up of T-34s leavened with some heavy tank units made up with heavier JS tanks. The Russians also mobilised élite Guards Tank armies, reminiscent of the days of the old Tsarist armies, to smash through the German lines.

Below: A rear view of a mid-production Panther Ausf A. Note the prominent commander's cupola which is located well to the rear of the turret, and the six *Schürzen* side skirting plates.

In January 1945, the thunder of Russian artillery marked the attack across the Vistula River. Once the German lines had been punctured, Russian armour raced through the gap to push deep behind the German lines. Some Russian tanks were equipped with a rudimentary form of Schnorkel gear which allowed amphibious crossings, and this enabled them to pass river obstacles such as the Vistula in the 1944 offensives.

The Germans fell back. Warsaw, the capital of Poland, soon fell to the tanks of the Red Army which were now advancing at a rate of 80.5km (50 miles) a day. However, Berlin was not taken in this advance and the advance on Berlin was not resumed until April 1945. The Russian Army's halt before Berlin has been the subject of hot debate. One explanation was the need to bring the logistical train forward to supply the men and tanks. Fuel was short and ammunition was needed to replenish the tanks, as well as guns. The usually reliable tanks within the Soviet tank armies suffered mechanical breakdowns, as with the Panther, and cut down on Soviet effectiveness, as the rapid advances took their toll on tracks and moving parts. There was also the question of the increasingly desperate German resistance in front of their capital. Units of every type – including Volkssturm units composed

Above: A Panther Ausf A with a traversed turret. The turret on a Panther Ausf A could traverse fully in only 15 seconds. Speed of traverse could mean the difference between life and death for the crew.

of the very old and very young – fought to halt the Soviet push on Berlin. German troops in Pomerania to the north also threatened any advance on Berlin with an attack into the Russians' flank. The early capture of Berlin was impossible.

OPERATION 'SPRING AWAKENING'

The Germans continued to organise a bitter rearguard action. In the west, this involved the Ardennes counter-offensive (Battle of the 'Bulge') in late 1944. The collapse of the 1944 Ardennes counter-offensive did not bring any respite for the battle-weary German troops and tank crews. In 1945, Hitler turned to the Waffen-SS formations of the Sixth SS Panzer Army for a new counter-offensive in the east. After a few days' rest and receipt of newly produced Panthers, he ordered the Sixth SS Panzer Army to Hungary to participate in the 10 February 1945 'Spring Awakening' offensive. The SS Hitlerjugend, for example, received 16 new Panther Ausf G tanks, raising its Panzer strength to 44. After four weeks' bitter, but futile, fighting in Hungary against overwhelming

Above: By 1945 the Soviet advance was unstoppable, and no amount of Panthers could have reversed the tide. Here Red Army troops move through the streets of Vienna.

Soviet forces, the division had lost 35 Panthers and fielded just nine operational Panzer V tanks.

THE BATTLE FOR THE SEELOW HEIGHTS AND GERMANY, 1945

The few Panthers which were left intact in the German armed forces were also in the thick of the action in the final desperate German efforts to prevent the fall of Berlin. During mid April 1945, the Panther tank fought its last major engagement in any strength. This was against Soviet armour which had broken through the German defences to advance across the Seelow Heights to Berlin. Here, for the last time, a battalion of Panthers – supported by some Tigers – savaged massed Soviet armour.

The battle for the Seelow Heights opened on 16 April when Russian searchlights illuminated the German positions for a pre-dawn attack. Their artillery and fighter bombers pounded the Germans in preparation for the assault. As the tanks moved forward, tanks and infantry were caught by the determined German defence. There was mayhem; even at this late stage of the war, when defeat was almost inevitable, the Germans still fought with fanatical determination. Around the Heights, one complete Panther battalion (as in the *bocage* of Normandy), proved itself a deadly adversary in

a defensive 'hull-down' position. After heavy fighting, the Russians forced the Germans off the Seelow Heights and advanced on Berlin

The Panthers were fighting a losing battle, and the Russians eventually crossed the Oder and Neisse rivers. In the towns on the road to Berlin, the Germans fought delaying actions. As at Stalingrad, tanks were at a disadvantage in urban warfare, and using Panzerfausts, the Germans quickly knocked out Russian tanks. Tank-busting teams, often comprised of Hitler Youth members, centred on an isolated Panther, Tiger or Panzer IV, and used Panzerfausts and explosive charges to take on the Russians. Frequently, the only weapon available to the Germans was the 'Molotov cocktail' petrol bomb which could set a Russian tank ablaze with a good shot. To counter this, Soviet tanks were accompanied into any built-up areas by teams of Russian infantry. In the end, however, the Germans were outnumbered and they fell back to fight a last desperate defence of the German capital.

THE BATTLE FOR BERLIN

The attack into Germany involved not just breaking the German lines centred on the Seelow Heights in front of Berlin, but also advancing into a built-up area encompassing hundreds of square miles of buildings, roads, sewers, tunnels and railways. Tanks were very vulnerable in city fighting, where determined infantry could hold up an armoured advance using roofs, windows and sewers to enfilade the tanks with petrol bombs, mines and Panzerfausts. At close ranges, and in the deadly environment of close-quarter fighting in areas like Berlin, the Russians needed to be wary. The battle for Berlin was going to be one of the hardest fought battles of the Eastern Front. By late April 1945, the Germans had been pushed back into the suburbs and centre of Berlin which had been pounded by Allied air forces during the war. The Russians added to the destruction as they advanced into the city with heavy artillery barrages. In fact, the rubble provided an excellent defence from which small, isolated German units held out.

To overcome the German defences inside Berlin, Russian tanks often took the expedient of driving through the buildings, thus avoid exposing themselves to any German infantry who might be waiting in the rubble. Civilian casualties were heavy; the Russians applied overwhelming firepower to their advance. Office and apartment blocks came crashing down as they pushed on to Hitler's bunker. By 27 April, they had reached Potsdamer Platz, just a few hundred yards from their goal. The last days of Hitler's supposed thousand-year Reich (which lasted a mere 12 years) were being played out in the ruins of Berlin.

As the Panther remained the principal weapon of Waffen-SS Panzer units until the end of the war, it was therefore fitting that small groups of SS Panthers – such as those fielded by the 11th SS Volunteer Panzergrenadier Division Nordland

– participated in the final, futile, defence of Berlin during April–May 1945. In one of the last Panther actions of the war, on 2 May 1945 the division's last two tanks spearheaded an attempt by the remnants of the encircled Berlin garrison to escape Soviet captivity. Even though both Panthers were destroyed, they helped create a tiny gap in the Soviet encirclement which allowed several hundred troops of the garrison to fight their way out west in order to surrender to the Americans.

Unlike the T-34 or the Sherman, the Panther did not see post-1945 service. It had been proof of the Germans' obsession with producing a quality tank while ignoring the question of numbers. As a result, the numbers of Allied Shermans and T-34s overcame the qualitatively superior Panther. In its one major action of the war, the battle of Kursk, the Panther failed to perform. Here lay the problem for the Germans during World War II: they produced too late a battle-winning weapon (such as the Panther) with little regard for how the limited numbers of such weapons would win the war. Eventually, it was a victory of tactics over strategy, and it would be grand strategy that would allow the Allies to win World War II.

Below: Soviet heavy tanks move into Berlin in April 1945. The numerical superiority of the Soviet armoured forces and the Allied air superiority ensured that the Panther was fighting a losing battle.

CHAPTER 5

Combat Performance: World War II Italian campaign, 1943–5

The mountainous terrain of Italy precluded large-scale tank operations. However, the terrain favoured the use of tanks in defensive 'hull down' position. The Germans took this advantage a step further by incorporating Panther turrets in fixed ground turret steel and concrete emplacements into their defensive lines which stretched across the Italian peninsula, thus incorporating the rugged terrain of Italy into their defensive lines to create formidable obstacles.

Under the overall command of the Luftwaffe Field Marshal, Albert Kesselring, the German forces in Italy planned to use these lines to make the Allied push upwards into Italy as costly as possible. The first of these lines encountered by the Allied forces was the 'Hitler line' along the coast south of Rome, and part of the more extensive 'Gustav line' stretching across the Italian 'boot'. The Gustav line included the infamous Monte Cassino Abbey, around which there were four bitter battles in 1944.

THE PANTHER GROUND TURRET

The Panther ground turret consisted of the standard Panther turret and its 75mm (2.9in) main gun armament (sometimes upgunned with an 88mm (3.46in) gun) mounted on top of a rectangular steel box dug into the ground. The box consisted of two parts. The upper portion was 332cm (131in) long, 283cm (111.5in) wide, and 97.7cm (38.5in) high, and incorporated the turret ball race and a manhole over an iron ladder down to a second section. This second compartment

Left: A Panther commander scans the horizon whilst sheltering in the lee of a ruined building on the Italian front. Visual reconnaissance like this was vital, particularly as the Germans lacked air superiority.

Above: A Panther Ausf D descending a bank in Italy. Few Panthers served in Italy, where the terrain was too rough for prolonged armoured operations.

conformed to the dimensions above but was 200cm (79in) high and further divided into three. One, lined with board, comprised a sleeping compartment for the gun crew and had an escape hatch; the second had the main access hatch and the ladder; the third was a storeroom for food and ammunition. The ground turret had electric light – provided from a battery in the storeroom – and fans to evacuate fumes. The whole gun turret was sunk into the ground to within a foot of the top of the upper section, and the spoil was built up to the base of the Panther turret and smoothed off in a long

ramp. The main access for the turret began some 12.2m (40ft) away and consisted of a slit trench sloping sharply downwards and covered at its deeper end with wooden beams and earth.

The ground turret is sometimes, mistakenly, referred to as the *Schmalturm* or 'small turret'. In fact, the *Schmalturm* was an experimental short turret fitted with a coincidence rangefinder. Trials with this turret were carried out using a Panther Ausf G chassis and the 'small turret' therefore should not be confused with the ground turret used in the Italian campaign.

Allied troops advancing up from the south first came across these Panther turrets in the German defences of the Hitler line south of Rome in 1944. In May 1944, British troops

Left: Panther turrets were used extensively on the defensive lines that the Germans established across Italy. Here a British soldier inspects a captured turret on the Gothic line in September 1944.

of the 5th Buffs and 8th Argylls received a rude shock when they attacked the Hitler line close by the town of Aquino. At dawn on 19 May, they moved forward through the early morning mist of the Liri valley. Steady progress was made through the German minefields until the mist cleared. The Canadian tanks supporting the attack then found themselves out in the open and looking down the barrel of a new type of German anti-tank weapon. These were not the normal towed or self-propelled guns. Earlier air reconnaissance had failed to interpret what was under the blobs of camouflage visible in the aerial photographs of the German defences.

ENCOUNTER ON THE HITLER LINE

Now the truth emerged. The blobs concealed Panther tank turrets mounted on a concrete emplacement, and covering all likely approaches through the minefields and ditches surrounding the town of Aquino. These turrets were manned by a specially trained company of the 15th Panzer Grenadier Division, the Panther Turret Company, made up entirely of men with considerable combat experience from fighting on the Eastern Front in the previous winter. Within minutes of the mist lifting, many of the Canadian Shermans were ablaze. Meanwhile, the accompanying Buffs and Argylls were engaged with heavy mortar and machine-gun fire from German support troops. Three Shermans of the leading troop of tanks were knocked out by one of the fixed Panther turrets, and the Allied advance against the Hitler line temporarily ground to a halt.

Further reconnaissance revealed how the Germans had used Panther turrets across their defensive lines to devastating effect. The strength of the German defences lay in their anti-tank defences, supported by a heavy concentration of artillery and nebelwerfer rockets. The anti-tank defences consisted of extensive minefields closely covered by anti-tank guns and infantry positions, and the anti-tank gun deployment was in a series of spearheads. At the tip of each spear was a Panther turret in a concrete emplacement. Echeloned behind, and in support of the Panther turret, were a further six towed or self-propelled anti-tank guns. In front of Aquino there were, all told, some 62 anti-tank guns covering a front of 7315m (8000yds). The only way to break such defences frontally was with heavy artillery assault followed by 'bite and hold' infantry assault. The infantry would have to work its way forward to knock out the Panther turrets with assault from the rear, while artillery and close tank support would provide fire support.

This, of course, was no easy task, and when the attack on Aquino resumed on 22 May, the attacking troops of the Princess Patricia's Canadian Light Infantry were soon held up by an unexpected minefield and fire from Panther turrets. More Panther turrets stopped a supporting tank squadron of the North Irish Horse, and so the infantry went on alone. Soon, however, communications gave out and control of the Patricias was lost. Two days later, some 30 men of the Patricias who had made it to the German wire returned to the regiment.

Meanwhile, the Seaforths, attacking in the centre, encountered similar problems to the Patricias. The tanks supporting the assault ran into a minefield and offered sitting targets to the Panther crews at close range. One gun destroyed 13 Churchill tanks before an armour-piercing round exploded its ammunition. The Seaforths, like the Patricias, pushed on alone without tank support but were unable to breach the German line. Towards the end of the battle, 41 out of 58 tanks on the 2 (Canadian) Brigade's front were knocked out in one day's fighting.

PANTHER VERSUS SHERMAN

When, on 24 May, the German positions on the Hitler line were turned by a flanking operation, the Germans deployed their first Panther tanks in the Western theatre in their conventional role, and not as turrets in concrete emplacements. In a short firefight, Canadian Shermans knocked out three Panthers, along with several self-propelled guns. This action is remarkable, considering the difficulties that Allied tanks such as the Sherman usually had when faced with a Panther.

Below: American infantrymen inspect a knocked-out Panther in Italy, 1944. The aperture for the 7.92mm (3.1in) co-axial machine gun is visible on the left hand side of the gun.

While some Shermans were upgunned, the Sherman was typically fitted with a 75mm gun which had a lamentable performance record against German Panthers and Tigers. This gun allowed the Sherman no penetration whatsoever at any range against the frontal amour of the Panther, even though the Panther's high velocity 75mm gun could blow apart a Sherman at ranges of 2743m (3000yds). The best chance for a Sherman was to hit a Panther in the side where it could penetrate at ranges of 3657m (4000yds). Having said this, the Panther could engage the Sherman in the flank at ranges up to 4572m (5000yds). Although the improved Sherman with its 76mm gun meant the tank had added punch, the Panther still had the advantage: a 76-mm gunned Sherman could penetrate the front turret of a Panther at 548m (600yds), but the Panther could do the same to the 76-mm Sherman at ranges of 2743m (3000yds).

It was in Normandy that extensive Sherman versus Panther engagements took place. In Italy, while Panthers were used in small numbers throughout the campaign in their normal role, it was their effectiveness in a fixed role which impressed the Germans. Their use in the Hitler line had undoubtedly made the line a tough position to break and had helped delay the Allied advance on Rome. The Germans, therefore, looked with interest at the Panther as they

planned their defence of the Italian peninsula north of Rome once the city had fallen to the Americans on 5 June 1944.

THE GOTHIC LINE

Further north, the Germans were building another defensive line to delay the Allied advance. This was the 'Gothic line' (called by the Allies the 'Pisa-Rimini line'), stretching from Pesaro on the Adriatic across the peninsula north of Florence to Massa on the Mediterranean. The Gothic line, like the Hitler line, made much use of Panther turrets. Its construction had been delayed by the construction of the Hitler and Gustav lines further south, but once these lines had been breached, the Germans worked frantically to finish it.

The Gothic line was a formidable obstacle. The Germans set about embedding Panther turrets, some with an 88mm gun, in steel and concrete bases. Close to the ground, these guns covered extensive fields of fire, whilst themselves being hard to hit. Surrounding the Panthers were hundreds of steel shelters for supporting infantry, along with rock tunnelling with carved defensive embrasures and deep minefields. The Gothic line made excellent use of the hilly terrain which lay cross-grained to the Allied advance. The effect was to carve across the Italian landscape an obstacle zone some 16.09km (10 miles) deep across which attacking Allied troops would have to pass. The Germans employed 15,000 Italian labourers to help build the line, with the whole operation supervised by the Todt Organisation. Having built the line, the Germans then created a 'free fire' zone by evacuating the local population across the construction zone.

Above: Concrete blocks have proved insufficient protection for this Panther. The Italian terrain favoured a static, defensive type of war for which the well-armoured Panther was a useful weapon.

What the Gothic line lacked were sufficient Panther turrets. The Germans worked hard to install the powerful turrets, but not all were in place when the Allies attacked in late 1944. Not withstanding this deficiency, the Gothic line was a tough nut to crack. Casualties were high as Allied troops advanced up the swept glacis and through the minefields of the Gothic line. German Panther turrets and anti-tank guns tore into the attacking Shermans, and German infantry quickly counter-attacked to push back any infantry which had advanced into the line. Eventually, at heavy cost, and with the Germans collapsing across Europe, the Allies breached the line in September 1944 and pushed on over the Apennine mountains to Northern Italy.

THE PANTHER IN ITALY

The Italian campaign, fought over hilly, close terrain, was very different from the fighting on the open steppes of the Eastern Front or the plains of France after the breakout from Normandy. It was not a campaign which favoured extensive tank action, but the Panther still proved itself in a defensive role, both in a hull down position, and as a gun turret fixed in concrete and steel. As ground turrets, the Panther was also used in the final stages of the war on the Eastern Front, the turrets being removed from damaged tanks to provide fixed defensive points in the final stages of the battle for Berlin.

CHAPTER 6

Combat Performance: World War II Normandy to Germany, 1944–5

Panther tanks also formed the mainstay of the German Army's efforts to resist the summer 1944 Allied invasion of Nazi-occupied France. During late 1943 and early 1944, the German Army in the West (the *Westheer*) strengthened its combat power and its Atlantic Wall coastal fortifications in order to defeat the imminently expected Allied invasion.

Field Marshal von Rundstedt, the German Commander-in-Chief in the West, fielded two subordinate army groups, including Field Marshal Rommel's Army Group B, which garrisoned the area the Allies would invade. Rommel's command included the Fifteenth Army in the Pas de Calais region, and Colonel-General Friedrich Dollman's Seventh Army, which protected Normandy and Brittany. In addition, von Rundstedt deployed a strategic armoured reserve, Panzer Group West. German strategy for repelling the Allies remained dogged by disagreement. Rommel wished to deploy his panzer divisions near to the coast to launch a quick counter-offensive against the invading Allies while they remained vulnerable. Other senior commanders wanted to hold back German armour to launch a decisive counter-offensive as the Allies subsequently attempted to push inland. The strategy the Germans ultimately adopted was a compromise between these two options and it pleased no one.

On 6 June 1944, the Westheer deployed nine panzer divisions and one panzergrenadier (mechanised) division, although many of these remained under strength. In total, the Westheer fielded 1513 AFVs that day, including 409 Panthers.

Left: A shot into the rear or side of a Panther was usually necessary for an Allied anti-tank gun to disable it. Here a Panther has been destroyed in a Normandy village in 1944.

Above: Panthers race to the Normandy beachhead in June 1944. Elite units like the SS and Panzer Lehr had priority on the latest equipment, such as the Panther, as it became available.

At this point, however, the Westheer fielded not a single operational Jagdpanther, which remained a very rare vehicle throughout the Normandy campaign: only 14 saw action. In fact, by 1 August 1944, only 47 of these vehicles had entered German service on any front.

On D-Day, 6 June 1944, the Allies landed along the Normandy coast despite poor weather. This decision caught the Germans off-guard, and on that critical first day, they responded tardily to the invasion. On 7 June, the Panzer IVs and Panthers of the 12th SS Hitlerjugend and 21st Panzer Divisions sought to push back into the sea the Anglo-Canadian forces which had landed. At the same time, von Rundstedt also rushed additional panzer divisions to the Normandy front line. During 7 June, General Bayerlein's Panzer Lehr Division, with its unusually large Panther tank contingent (some 90 vehicles strong), advanced to the front, only to suffer heavily at the hands of Allied tactical air power. On 9 June the I SS Panzer Corps (which included the Lehr, 12th SS Hitlerjugend, and 21st Panzer Divisions) went onto the defensive. German strategy now changed from one of

repulsing the invasion to a policy of containment. Hence, all along a front line stretching from south-east of Bayeux to north-east of Caen, German tank crews dug-in their Panzer IVs and Panthers and carefully camouflaged them.

During the rest of June, the Germans continued to rush additional armoured units to the front in preparation for another major offensive. By late June 1944, the II SS Panzer

Corps had reached the bridgehead after being transferred to France from the Eastern Front. While the II SS Corps completed its redeployment, German forces strove to hold their positions in the face of repeated Allied attacks in order to deny the latter room for manoeuvre. On 12 June, however, British armour penetrated the German panzer screen in front of Caen. However, as the British 7th Armoured Division pushed south the next day, a German armoured riposte at Villers Bocage smashed the British spearhead. One dozen Tiger tanks of the 101st SS Heavy Tank Battalion, commanded by SS-Obersturmführer (Lieutenant) Michael Wittman, left

Below: Panthers rest in a French town on the way to the Normandy bocage. Note how the two tanks have formed up covering each other's rear, the most vulnerable part of a Panther.

40 British vehicles burning on the battlefield. This success enabled the Germans to rebuild their shattered positions to the west and north of Caen.

By late June, another powerful armoured force had arrived at the front: the 2nd SS Panzer Division Das Reich. This formation had commenced its journey to Normandy from southern France as early as 8 June 1944, but its progress had

been delayed by attacks launched by the French resistance. With its commitment to the front, the defending German forces were augmented by a further 51 Panthers. With this division arrived one of the best-known Waffen-SS tank aces of the entire war, SS NCO Ernst Barkmann. After establishing his combat prowess with Ausf A Panthers in the East during autumn 1943, Barkmann went on to command a Ausf G Panther in the 4th Company, 2nd SS Panzer Regiment.

EPSOM

On 24 June 1944, Rommel began planning an armoured counter-stroke which he hoped would force the Allies back into the Channel. By then, SS-Oberstgruppenführer (Col-Gen) Hausser's II Panzer Corps had detrained in eastern France and would soon reach the front. Late on 28 June, Hausser's Corps, including 80 Panthers plus 90 Panzer IVs, reached the front around Caen. Unfortunately for the Germans, Allied 'Ultra' intelligence had forewarned General Montgomery of the arrival of Hausser's Corps. Montgomery launched his own offensive, Operation 'Epsom', to force Rommel to commit his SS armour instead of assembling it in reserve as a counter-offensive force. 'Epsom' involved an attack by General Richard O'Connor's VIII Corps west of Caen which aimed to push south-east across the Odon valley to threaten Caen from the south. O'Connor's forces accomplished an advance to the Odon, which forced Rommel to assemble Hausser's SS Panzer Corps on 29 June for a counter-stroke. However, as Hausser's Corps assembled, concentrated Allied naval and artillery fire smashed the two SS divisions and between them, they lost 19 Panthers. Hausser's Corps began its counter-stroke the next day but made only limited progress.

After the failure of Hausser's intended offensive, German strategy reverted to containing the Allied bridgehead in an attempt to deny them the terrain and room required for decisive mobile operations. On 10 July, German forces abandoned their positions north of Caen, and instead concentrated on creating a powerful defensive system south of Caen which protected the open countryside south of the Bourguébus ridge. By 18 July, Army Group B had established a dispersed defensive system which incorporated five defence lines.

GOODWOOD

On 18 July 1944, Montgomery launched his 'Goodwood' offensive. It was designed to outflank Caen to the east by using the three armoured divisions of O'Connor's VIII Corps. Unknown to the Allies, these forces struck the deepest German defensive system so far established in Normandy. Prior to the ground attack, massive Allied artillery and aerial strikes smashed the forward German defences, thereby enabling the British 11th Armoured Division to push forward rapidly on that first morning. However, the preliminary Allied strikes barely touched the deeper German positions on the

Bourguébus ridge, including the 49 Panthers of the 1st SS Leibstandarte Division. That afternoon, as the 11th Armoured drove forward, local German tank reserves launched small counter-strokes to buy time while SS Panther companies assembled on the rear slope of the Bourguébus ridge for a major counter-blow. This operation, launched that evening, decimated the British armoured spearhead. Although 'Goodwood' continued until 20 July, German Panthers and Tigers had already managed to stem the Allied advance by the night of 18/19 July.

AMERICAN BREAKOUT

While Montgomery conducted 'Goodwood', the Americans started planning for a major offensive, Operation 'Cobra', which sought to capitalise on the German forces being sucked into the Caen area by the British offensive. On 26 July, General Bradley commenced 'Cobra' with concentrated strategic bombing attacks. They inflicted massive casualties on the already battered Panzer Lehr Division; by the evening of 27 July, the Lehr had only five Panthers still operational. During the first 48 hours of 'Cobra', the Americans smashed through the German defences and advanced south. One individual who played a prominent role in the desperate efforts made by the SS Das Reich Division to stem this advance was Ernst Barkmann, who by this time had already accomplished 10 tank 'kills' in Normandy. On 26 June, Barkmann's Panther fought several fierce engagements with American Sherman tanks, before his vehicle succumbed to mechanical failure. German mechanics repaired the vehicle overnight, and next day, Barkmann's Panther resumed its defensive actions against the Americans. However, the Allied advance that day cut Barkmann off from the rest of the 4th Company. The SS NCO continued to engage American forces single-handedly, accounting for another eight enemy vehicles in a single day, before major damage – sustained after several Allied hits – forced the tank to limp away south to safety.

Despite isolated successes, like that of Barkmann, the still-powerful SS Das Reich Division failed woefully to stem the Allied advance. One reason for this poor performance was the collapsing German logistic system. Since D-Day, the Allied aerial interdiction plan had smashed the German transportation system in Normandy, thus seriously degrading German capability to resupply front line units with fuel and ammunition. Consequently, by 26 July, German fuel and ammunition stocks in the 'Cobra' sector had sunk critically low. These shortages forced the 2nd SS Division to abandon two entire companies of valuable Panther tanks, and prevented it from employing the mobile counter-strike methods which had proved effective during 'Goodwood'.

By 29 June, American forces had advanced 48km (30 miles) to Avranches at the foot of the Normandy peninsula, in the face of crumbling German resistance. Even the heroic resistance offered by Ernst Barkmann had ended by this date; he was forced to abandon his burning Panther and spent the

Above: Two Panther Ausf As knocked out in the Normandy bocage. In these Normandy hedgerows tank engagements took place at very close quarters.

next three days fighting his way on foot out of an American encirclement. By capturing Avranches on 29 June, the Americans were capable of immediately breaking out of Normandy in all directions. Into this hole in the German front, the Americans fed the armoured divisions of General Patton's Third Army. These forces rapidly fanned out to race deep into the heart of France against minimal German resistance.

BLUECOAT

After the Americans had managed to break through the German defences in 'Cobra', British forces attempted, in Operation 'Bluecoat', to widen this 48.3km (30 miles) breach in the German front. The British struck south from Caumont toward Vire and Vassy, and the battered German units in the area fell back as they could not halt the British advance. However, on 30 July the Germans achieved one notable tactical success when a company of newly arrived

Jagdpanthers, the tank destroyer variant of the Panther, entered combat in the West for the first time. On D-Day, the 654th Army Heavy Anti-tank Battalion, deployed near Paris, was undertaking crew familiarisation training with their newly delivered Jagdpanthers. By late July 1944, only one company of these vehicles was ready for action, and thus the unit was committed to halt the 'Bluecoat' offensive. On 30 June, the 654th's 2nd Company blunted the momentum of the British advance. That morning, the British 15th (Scottish) Division, plus the 6th Guards Tank brigade, broke through the German defences line and advanced towards Hill 309. Then three Jagdpanthers, waiting in concealed positions, ambushed a squadron of Churchill tanks. In a brief encounter, the German vehicles knocked out 11 Churchills before heavy British fire forced them to withdraw, leaving two damaged Jagdpanthers abandoned on the battlefield. Despite this local success for the Germans, however, British armour continued to drive south until they captured Vire in early August.

Below: A wrecked Panther entangled with a telephone wire being inspected by an Allied soldier. The deep ditches and high hedgerows are typical of the Norman countryside.

Above: Panzergrenadiers prepare for an Allied attack in Normandy while a Panther covers them. Panthers would rarely remain this exposed to air attack for long.

MORTAIN

As American armour raced in all directions beyond Avranches into France, the only realistic German response was a general retreat behind the River Seine. Instead Hitler ordered his forces to initiate a counter-offensive, Operation 'Lüttich', from the Mortain area. In this counter-blow, the XLVII Panzer Corps thrust toward Avranches to encircle and smash the dozen American divisions which had already burst out beyond Avranches. The German Army scraped together the battered remnants of six mobile divisions into an armoured strike force which fielded 250 tanks, including some 95 Panthers. This force also received fuel supplies for a few days of sustained offensive action, though only by halting supplies to other parts of the Normandy front.

On the night of 6/7 August 1944, the 185 Panzer IVs and Panthers of XLVII Corps attacked toward Avranches. However, as American reserves reached the area, the German advance stalled, with particularly heavy losses within its Panther companies. The inevitable failure of the Mortain offensive only made a terrible German situation worse, since it pushed much of the remaining German armour further

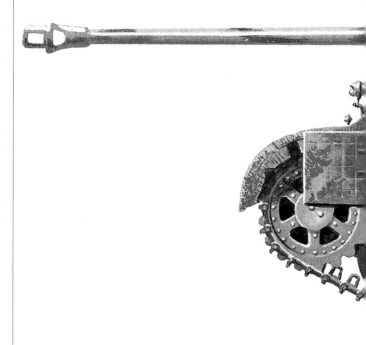

west and deeper into the noose of a sizeable Allied pocket beginning to form in the Mortain-Argentan area.

TOTALIZE

Despite their failure at Mortain, German Panthers enjoyed more success in their attempts to stem further Allied offensives south of Caen. In early August General Simonds' II Canadian Corps commenced planning for Operation 'Totalize', which sought to push south from the Bourguébus area to meet up with the Americans who had broken out at Avranches and were advancing north toward Argentan. It was obvious to the Germans that if 'Totalize' successfully joined up with the Americans, some 20 German divisions would be encircled in the Falaise area. To prevent this, they maintained powerful defences south of Caen. During the early hours of 8 August, Canadian armour advanced south after a preliminary heavy bomber attack. Despite their swift penetration of the initial German defences, Simonds still ordered his forces to pause for a second bombing strike on the next German defensive zone. Unfortunately, this allowed the German defenders time to reorganise their positions.

As part of this next phase of the offensive, a Canadian battle group named Worthington Force advanced to seize Hill

195. However, the force got lost during the night of 8/9 August and at dawn, two small SS tank detachments, built around a nucleus of just 15 Panthers, attacked and decimated the isolated Canadian force. Indeed, by the evening of 9 August, the Germans had successfully utilised their meagre armoured battle groups to halt the 'Totalize' offensive. Subsequently, during a four-day period from 14 August, the Germans conducted a fighting withdrawal in face of Operation 'Tractable', the second Canadian attempt to capture Falaise.

THE FALAISE POCKET

The Canadians did not capture Falaise until 18 August, by which date the remnants of 20 German divisions were streaming east in an attempt to escape the Allied pincers closing in on Trun. After Canadian and American forces had closed the Falaise pocket on 19 August, the Germans launched the few remaining Panthers of the II SS Panzer Corps from outside the pocket in an attempt to smash an

Below: A Panther on which the *Zimmerit* anti-magnetic mine paste can clearly be seen. This was abandoned late in the war, when the days needed for the paste to dry could not be spared by the Germans.

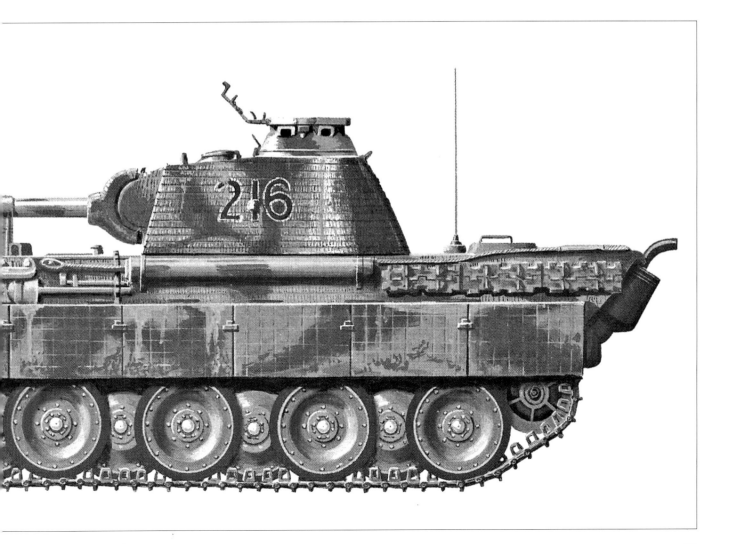

Above: Two generations of panzer knocked out in Normandy. In the foreground is the tank the Panther was designed to replace, the Pzkfw IV. The wider tracks of the Panther can clearly be seen.

escape route through to the encircled German troops. At the same time, improvised battlegroups attempted to fight their way out from inside the pocket. The Allied plug held its ground against these desperate efforts, and only several dozen small German combat teams managed to fight their way out of an inferno which later became known as the Hell of Falaise. In total, just 35,000 Germans troops out of the 100,000 in the Falaise area managed to escape encirclement and destruction. Precious little heavy equipment escaped, however; the SS Das Reich, for instance, failed to extricate a single working Panther from the pocket.

By 23 August, the Allies had overcome the last remaining enemy resistance in the pocket, and now the battered remnants of Army Group B faced the prospect of being caught in a larger Allied pocket in front of the Seine. To avoid a second Falaise pocket, the Germans raced backwards – both day and night – to cross the river before the Allies crossed it. A large proportion of the three dozen Panthers the Germans had extricated from Falaise either succumbed to Allied air attacks on the way to the Seine, or were abandoned due to fuel

shortages. Some of the few Panthers which reached the river failed to get across, despite desperate ferrying operations under heavy Allied fire. Two Jagdpanthers of the 654th's 2nd Company, however, proved highly fortunate, surmounting all these risks and making it back across the Seine at Elbeuf. By the time the Allies had raced across the Seine, the Westheer had been reduced to perhaps 60 tanks, including no more than 15 Panthers. The Westheer's armoured forces had ceased to exist, and nothing could stop the Allies as they raced through France, into Belgium and on to the very borders of the Reich. Only logistic over-stretch saved the Germans from an even greater catastrophic disaster in the west during August and September 1944.

THE ARDENNES

Another well-known German operation in the West in which Panthers featured prominently was the battle of the Bulge, the German December 1944 Ardennes counter-offensive. On 16 September 1944, after the Allied advance had stalled short of the Reich, Hitler decided to launch a German counter-offensive in the Ardennes in mid-December, which would – despite the unfavourable battlefield situation – regain the strategic initiative in the West and seize the vital port of Antwerp. The Germans earmarked Field Marshal Model's

Left: German panzers in a French field attempt to evade an Allied air attack. Tanks that remained this exposed soon became victims of the Allied fighter-bombers.

Below: German tanks including Panthers knocked-out in France. It appears from the shell-holes and damaged trees that they were caught in a bombardment of some kind.

Army Group B to carry out the counter-offensive, spear-headed by SS-Oberstgruppenführer (Col-Gen) Dietrich's Sixth Panzer Army and General Hasso von Manteuffel's Fifth Panzer Army. The Germans opted to attack in the hilly, rugged, and heavily wooded Ardennes, since its unsuitability for offensive operations led the Americans to defend this sec-

Below: Panthers on the offensive, as they advance during the German winter campaign in the Ardennes in 1944. These tanks probably belong to the Sixth SS Panzer Army.

tor with just four divisions. Though Hitler demanded that Model's forces advance 153km (95 miles) north-west to seize Antwerp and cut Montgomery's divisions off from the American forces deployed to the south, every German commander involved in the operation insisted that his forces were too small to achieve such an ambitious objective. In particular, the logistic basis for such an offensive remained woefully inadequate, with the Germans especially short of fuel. Indeed, the attack plan required that German armour capture Allied fuel dumps in order to continue the attack.

In total, the Germans committed approximately 950 armoured fighting vehicles, including about 340 Panthers and 49 Jagdpanthers. Dietrich's Sixth Panzer Army was spearheaded by the I SS Panzer Corps, commanded by SS-Gruppenführer (Lt-Gen) Preiss. It included the 1st and 12th SS Panzer Divisions Leibstandarte and Hitlerjugend and in addition, Dietrich's command included SS-Gruppenführer (Lt-Gen) Wilhelm Bittrich's II SS Panzer Corps which fielded the 2nd SS and 9th SS Panzer Divisions Das Reich and Hohenstaufen. To the south, Hasso von Manteuffel's Fifth Panzer Army was spearheaded by the LVIII Panzer Corps with the 116th Panzer Division, and by General Heinrich von Lüttwitz's XXXXVII Panzer Corps, which deployed the 2nd and Lehr Panzer Divisions.

Despite desperate German efforts to rebuild these seven spearhead panzer divisions, on 16 December 1944 all remained under strength. Instead of fielding the standard two-battalion armoured regiment with about 140 tanks, five of these divisions fielded instead a single organic armoured battalion, with a mixture of 66 Panzer IVs together with two Panther companies each of 14 vehicles, plus four command variants, making a total of 62 Panthers committed to the fray. To make up for the absent second tank battalion, the German Army allocated each of these divisions with a formerly independent armoured battalion equipped with StuG IIIs, Jagdpanzer IVs or Jagdpanthers. For example, to the Panzer

Lehr Division, the Germans attached the 559th Army Heavy Anti-tank Battalion.

The remaining two panzer divisions – the SS Das Reich and 116th – retained the standard 1944 establishment. Their armoured regiments each included one mixed battalion of Panzer IVs and assault guns, together with a Panther battalion of 56 vehicles, plus four command variants. None of the divisions involved in the offensive, however, reached these theoretical establishments. In theory, these seven panzer divisions – according to these establishments – ought to have fielded 490 Panthers, but in reality, due to shortages, no more than 340 actually participated. The 2nd Panzer Division, for example, fielded just 28 Panthers out of a theoretical establishment of 60 such vehicles.

In addition, the Germans also fielded 49 Jagdpanthers, representing one seventh of the total number of this model ever produced. These heavy tank destroyers were deployed in one of three companies within the independent Army Heavy Anti-tank Battalions. The Germans deployed six such battalions in the Ardennes, either as independent units, or as substitutes for the missing second tank battalion of certain panzer divisions. Like all of the German forces involved on the

Below: A thoroughly wrecked Panther that has been used by the Allies for target practice. The entry holes of the shells are clearly visible in the front armour plate.

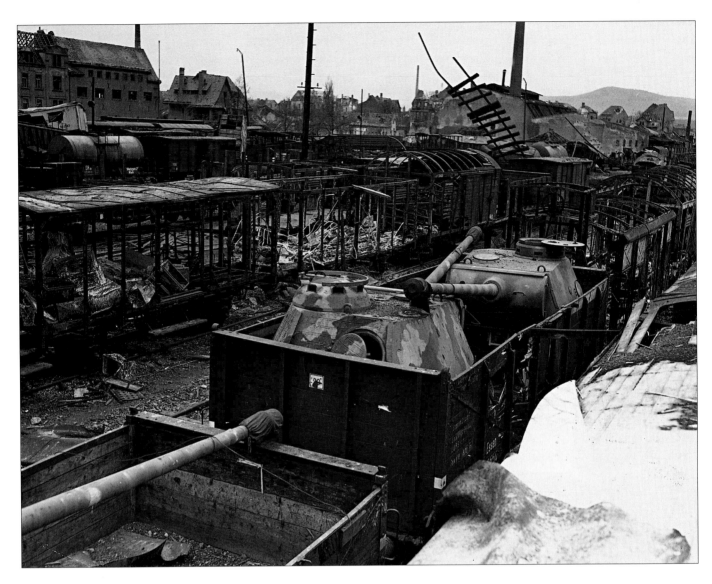

Above: An Allied bombing raid on these railyards has damaged Panther turrets awaiting delivery as well as much of the local area. Raids like this greatly hindered the German war effort.

Ardennes, these six battalions remained significantly under strength; out of a theoretical establishment of 84 Jagdpanthers, only 49 actually participated in the offensive.

To improve their prospects of success, the Germans adopted special measures for their counter-strike. Firstly, acutely aware that Allied aerial superiority emasculated their tactical mobility, the Germans only attacked during a pre-dicted period of sustained bad weather which kept back Allied tactical aircraft. Secondly, the Germans undertook a special mission intended to facilitate the momentum of their attack. Hitler ordered SS-Standartenführer (Colonel) Otto Skorzeny's 150th Panzer Brigade to sow confusion behind American lines. Skorzeny's troops, some dressed in American Military Police uniforms, infiltrated through American posi-tions to misdirect Allied traffic, while 12 Panthers, cleverly disguised as American M-10 tank destroyers, attacked American forces. The Germans gained only limited benefit

from this subterfuge, however, and once Skorzeny's forces lost the element of surprise, they soon suffered heavy casu-alties, including all 12 disguised Panthers.

Early on 16 December 1944, Dietrich's Sixth Panzer Army launched its offensive from east of the Elsenborn ridge and thrust north-west toward the River Meuse bridges south of Liège. Dietrich's advance was spearheaded by the *Kampfgruppe Peiper*, a reinforced armoured regiment from the SS *Leibstandarte* Division. Led by SS-Obersturmbann-führer (Lt-Col) Joachim Peiper, the battle group fielded Panzer IV and Panther tanks and was to advance rapidly toward Antwerp before the Allies reacted. Behind Peiper's forces advanced an attached SS battalion with 30 King Tiger tanks. These massive vehicles were unsuited to Peiper's designated mission of advancing quickly along a few narrow roads in poor terrain, and they soon fell behind Peiper's spearhead Panther tanks.

During 17–19 December, Peiper's Panther and Panzer IV tanks advanced 40km (25 miles) to Stoumont. But at this point, Allied resistance halted Peiper's advance, and by 22 December eve, some of his cumbersome King Tigers had caught up with his now stalled spearhead Panthers. On 20 December, with Peiper's advance halted, the Germans sought to develop new axes of advance to maintain the momentum of the offensive. Dietrich entrusted this task to the SS Hitlerjugend Division, which he ordered to smash the Allied positions at Dom Bütgenbach. The SS Hitlerjugend committed the 33 tank destroyers fielded by the attached 560th Army Heavy Anti-tank Battalion, which was standing in for the division's missing second tank battalion. Some 25 Jagdpanzer IV/70s and eight Jagdpanthers provided fire support for the frenzied attacks which the fanatical motorised infantrymen of the *Hitlerjugend* launched against the Allied positions at Dom Bütgenbach. Although this attack proved successful, the SS Hitlerjugend subsequently proved unable to restore the momentum of the stalled northern thrust.

On 21 December, when Allied counter-attacks had surrounded Peiper's troops at La Gleize and cut them off from their supplies, Peiper's force was down to just 40 AFVs, including 15 Panthers and seven King Tigers. By the night of 23/24 December, Peiper's force had ran out of fuel and ammunition and attempted to escape out of its encirclement on foot. The force abandoned its remaining 35 tanks, including 14 Panthers, and disabled them to avoid their falling intact into Allied hands. After the destruction of Peiper's force, the northern thrust undertaken by the well-equipped, SS-dominated, Sixth Panzer Army degenerated into a costly failure.

To the south, General Manteuffel's Fifth Panzer Army also commenced their attacks at dawn on 16 December 1944. Despite fierce American resistance at St Vith, both his two panzer corps advanced 32km (20 miles) towards Houffalize and Bastogne during the first 48 hours. During 18 December, Panzer IV and Panther tanks of the 2nd Panzer Division skirted around Bastogne, and drove west toward the Meuse bridges near Dinant. Late on that same day, the Panther spearheads of the Panzer Lehr Divisions reached Bastogne, and by 21 December, German forces had encircled the American garrison at Bastogne. The day of 23 December constituted the high point of the German offensive, when Panthers of the 2nd Panzer Division advanced to within sight of the Meuse bridges. However, having failed to capture sufficient Allied fuel stocks, these Panthers ran out of petrol and the German thrust stalled.

On 23 December, American forces attacked north-east against Manteuffel's positions to relieve their forces encircled at Bastogne, which they duly reached on 26 December. By now Germans commanders had concluded that continuing the attack was pointless, but Hitler insisted that on New Year's Day, 1945, Manteuffel's Army – now reinforced by the I SS Panzer Corps – undertake one final attack around Bastogne to snatch success out of the jaws of defeat.

To facilitate this renewed attack, Hitler instructed the Westheer to launch a diversionary offensive in Alsace-Lorraine on New Year's Eve 1944. In Operation 'Northwind', six German divisions thrust south toward Strasbourg to meet a southern pincer launched from the Colmar Pocket, a German-held salient which jutted west beyond the River Rhine on to French soil. One of the armoured spearheads of this operation was provided by the eight Jagdpanthers and 15 Jagdpanzer IVs of the 654th Army Heavy Anti-tank Battalion. In late December 1944, the Germans redeployed this unit from reserve positions behind the Ardennes front to the Lorraine sector. The Germans had intended that the two pincers involved in 'Northwind' would meet at Strasbourg, for they hoped that this threat to a French town which was imbued with such symbolic significance would force a redeployment of Allied forces away from the Ardennes to Alsace-Lorraine.

The 654th Battalion's eight operational Jagdpanthers spearheaded the advance undertaken by the southern German pincer, during which it lost half of its Jagdpanthers. These heavy tank destroyers rarely succumbed to Allied fire, thanks to their low silhouettes and well-sloped armour. But Jagdpanthers remained vulnerable to disablement through damage to their tracks, or through mechanical failure. During the operation, the Germans lost one Jagdpanther to engine failure, while another was abandoned after track damage. In addition, at Wolfgantzen on 6 February 1945, the Battalion lost another Jagdpanther when French forces destroyed both of its tracks. The German vehicle had taken up an ambush position in a small wood, but instead was itself surprised by Sherman tanks of the First French Army. Two columns of Shermans engaged the Jagdpanther from either flank and destroyed its tracks, forcing the German crew to abandon the vehicle. Furthermore, a fourth Jagdpanther was abandoned after engine failure, but a Bergepanther armoured recovery vehicle managed to tow the stricken vehicle back to a German depot to be repaired at a later date. Overall, the operation failed to captured Strasbourg, and managed to divert only a few American units away from the battle of the Bulge.

Due to the failure of 'Northwind' to pull away sizeable Allied forces from the Ardennes, when the renewed German thrust in the latter area commenced, it achieved only minor success in the face of increasing Allied strength. On 3 January 1945, the Allies attacked the Fifth Panzer Army and, over the next two weeks, gradually forced the Germans back to their original starting positions. During one month's combat in the Ardennes, Model's forces lost 600 AFVs (including 190 Panthers) and 120,000 troops, all of which were irreplaceable. Now only battered remnants stood between the Allies and a successful advance across the River Rhine into the heart of the Reich. With hindsight, it is clear that the German Ardennes counter-offensive was a futile gamble which wasted Germany's last armoured reserves. By late 1945, the failure of the operation ensured that it would only be a matter of months before Nazi Germany inevitably succumbed to defeat by the Allies.

CHAPTER 7

Panther Variants

The costly experience the Germans gained at Kursk with the new Panther Ausf D tank convinced them that in its current configuration, the vehicle was unfit for combat, and this led them to undertake extensive modifications to the tank. However, the basic design – gun, hull and turret layout, plus armour distribution – remained the same.

The Panther Ausf A was the first variant; the modifications included a new cast cupola (which both improved the commander's protection and field of vision), plus 5mm- (0.19in) thick side skirts to protect the tracks from enemy hollow-charge weapons. This vehicle was distinguishable from its predecessor by its ball-mounted bow machine gun which gave a wider field of fire. Other design modifications included strengthened road wheels to counteract the overloading of the suspension, and an improved transmission and gearbox. At the same time, introduction of additional cooling pipes and the abandonment of watertight sealing reduced the Panther's susceptibility to engine fires, which had crippled so many vehicles at Kursk. These changes raised the vehicle's weight to 44 tonnes (43.3 tons). Finally, from September 1943, the Germans applied Zimmerit anti-magnetic mine paste to the tank to protect it from magnetic anti-tank mines. Production of the Ausf A commenced during late summer 1943 and continued until summer 1944. In total, the German firms Daimler-Benz, Henschel, MAN, and MNH constructed 1768 Ausf A Panthers during 1943–44 at an average rate of 150 vehicles per month.

During autumn 1943, as sizeable numbers of Ausf A Panthers began to enter German service, Hitler decided that each panzer division would received an entire battalion of Panther tanks to replace their current Panzer III-equipped battalion. In theory, this Panther battalion fielded 76 Panther tanks: four companies each with 17 standard vehicles, plus a headquarters staff company with a further eight Panthers, including three command variants. In addition, the panzer regiment's staff company possessed a further three com-

Left: A column of formidable Jagdpanthers cross a plain, possibly on a training exercise. This view emphasises the 88mm (3.46in) gun which was a potent tank killing weapon.

87

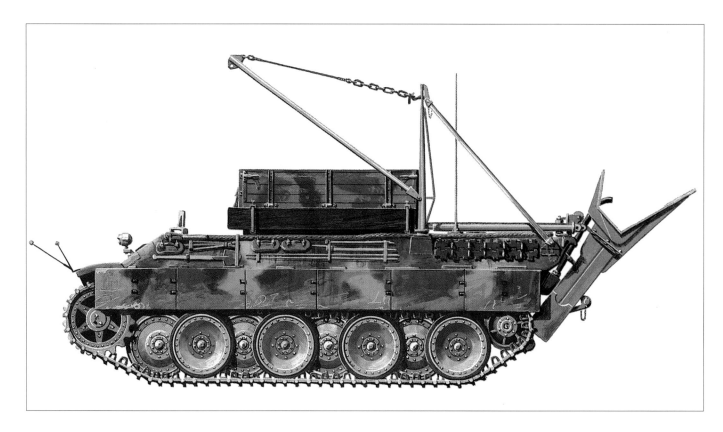

Above: A *Bergepanther* recovery vehicle, a number of which were made by Henschel to try to keep the German panzer armies functioning and serviceable towards the end of the war.

mand Panthers, bringing the theoretical divisional total to 79 Panthers, including the six command variants.

During 1943–44, German panzer divisions returned one armoured battalion to Germany where they re-equipped with the Panther Ausf A and then underwent field trials before returning to their parent formation. The 1st Panzer Division was the first formation to be so re-equipped, while the first Waffen-SS division to do so was the 2nd SS Panzer Division *Das Reich*. By January 1944 some 15 panzer divisions fielded a Panther battalion equipped with Ausf A vehicles, a theoretical inventory of 1150 tanks. Even though a newer version, the Ausf G, superseded the Ausf A, the latter continued to spearhead German resistance to the Allies for the rest of the war.

PANTHER MODEL G

In early 1944, the German High Command became concerned about the delays experienced in the development programme for the Panther's replacement, the Panther II. Hitler ordered that the modifications already developed for the Panther II be incorporated into a new version of the standard Panther designated the Ausf G. The first of these rolled off German production lines in February 1944. The four firms involved in Panther production increasingly switched from construction of the Ausf A to that of the Ausf G, joined later by a fifth firm, DEMAG. Mass production of the Ausf G com-

menced during spring 1944 and continued until the war's end. These firms built 3740 Panther Ausf G tanks during 1944–45, and monthly production peaked in August 1944, before raw material shortages and Allied bombing reduced production to 25 vehicles a month by spring 1945.

The Panther Ausf G encompassed a major redesign of the hull which introduced sloped rather than vertical armour plates on the lower hull sides, and more steeply sloped armour elsewhere. In addition, upper side armour was thickened from 40mm (1.6in) to 50mm (2in). This redesign enhanced armour shot deflection capabilities, simplified production, and improved use of available space, allowing main armament stowage to be increased from 79 to 82 rounds. The first SS formation to receive large numbers of Ausf G Panthers was the 5th SS Panzer Division Wiking. In spring 1944, both the division's panzer battalions were re-equipped entirely with a total of 160 Panthers whilst in reserve in Poland. In July 1944, the rebuilt Wiking Division was again committed to combat in the East in a desperate attempt to stem the rapid advances made by the Soviet 'Bagratian' offensive in White Russia.

From May 1944, other Wehrmacht and SS divisions progressively received Ausf G Panthers to replace lost Ausf As. The Ausf G continued to spearhead German defensive efforts right up to the last weeks of the war. By this time, development of the Panther II was far advanced, but the deteriorating battlefield situation precluded commencement of production. Instead, German firms included extra features of the Panther II – such as all-steel road wheels – into late production Panther Ausf G vehicles.

COMMAND PANTHER

As well as the standard combat tank, German firms also manufactured a command tank variant, designated the Sdkfz 167. In total, 500 Panther command tanks were built between early 1943 and March 1945. These vehicles proved superior to previous German command tanks in that they retained their main armament. German 1944 panzer division establishments included six command Panthers, although actual numbers fielded often fell below this authorised number. The Command Panther carried two types of powerful communications systems. It mounted the standard Fu 5 radio located in the turret with a 2m (79in) rod antenna, which produced an effective range of 8km (5m). In addition, the vehicle also carried in its hull a long range Fu 8 radio supported by a 1.3m (51in) star antenna mounted on the rear deck, which could operate up to distances of 65km (40 miles).

Initially, only the German factories could convert standard Panthers into command variants, but from July 1944, all new Panthers incorporated features which permitted formation workshops to convert standard tanks into command versions in the field. This development eased the difficulties the Germans experienced in replacing destroyed command vehicles, but did not alleviate fully the ensuing shortages. Not even the favoured Waffen-SS always enjoyed a full complement of Command Panthers; on D-day, for instance, the 12th SS Panzer Division *Hitlerjugend* fielded just four such vehicles. Overall, the Panther command tank proved a useful machine, not just because it retained its main gun, but also because it resembled its sister battle tank and thus the enemy found it difficult to identify and target these important battlefield assets.

BERGEPANTHER RECOVERY VEHICLE

The first German experience in the art of recovering damaged Ausf D Panthers from the battlefield gained at Kursk made it clear that they needed a powerful fully tracked recovery vehicle. The substantial Panther chassis constituted the obvious choice, but initially the rush to get the Ausf D tank into service delayed efforts to design such a vehicle. Despite these delays, in June 1943 the firm of MAN dispatched 12 Ausf D Panthers (less their turrets) direct from the factory for use as towing vehicles with the two Panther battalions earmarked to spearhead the Kursk offensive. Subsequently, Henschel designed and produced some 70 *Bergepanther* recovery tanks during July–August 1943. This vehicle utilised the basic Panther chassis but instead of a turret, it mounted a 40 tonne (39.4 ton) winch powered by the tank's electrical turret traverse system. Some basic protection was provided for the crew by an open wood and steel superstructure with a canvas roof cover. A heavy earth spade was also hinged at the rear plate for use as a counterbalance. The *Bergepanther* proved a highly effective recovery vehicle, not least because it was powerful enough to recover the

Above: Crew members inside a Jagdpanther, whose main armament made the interior rather cramped. The loading or escape hatch and shells ready to be loaded can clearly be seen.

heavier Tiger tank. Its armoured chassis helped protect the crew from enemy fire and, as the war dragged on, German forces were compelled increasingly to attempt the recovery of damaged vehicles even under direct enemy fire. In total, MAN and Henschel built some 350 *Bergepanthers*, sufficient to equip each Panther battalion with at least two vehicles.

NIGHT-FIGHTING PANTHER

During early 1944, the Germans also equipped a very small number of Panthers with a 300mm (11.8in) *Uhu* (Owl) infrared searchlight and an image converter. However, these searchlights only possessed an effective range of 600m (650yds), which virtually negated the benefit of the Panther's excellent long-range 75mm gun. In mid-1944, therefore, the Germans mounted a more powerful infrared searchlight on a half-track which would deploy close to the night-fighting Panther to provide better illumination. These two vehicles served with a third one to form a combat team known as Sparrowhawk. This third vehicle was a half-track carrying a panzergrenadier squad and equipped with assault rifles due to be fitted with night-sights. The Sparrowhawk team were capable, at least in theory, of engaging night-time targets as far away as 2500m (2750yds).

During mid-1944, one company of the 116th Panzer Division re-equipped with night-fighting Panthers, but it is not clear if they ever saw combat. This is also true of a solitary Sparrowhawk Panther team deployed to Hungary in January 1945 for the 'Awakening of Spring' offensive intended to relieve the Budapest garrison. However, on 21 April 1945, two night-fighting Panthers with the improvised Panzer Division Clausewitz overran American anti-tank positions near the Weser-Elbe Canal, in the only confirmed combat by Sparrowhawk teams. A few more sophisticated night-fighting Panthers, known as Solution-B vehicles, were converted in the last weeks of the war from old Ausf A and D panthers. In these vehicles, unlike the Sparrowhawk versions, both commander and gunner enjoyed night-fighting capabilities. In April 1945 the Panzer Division Clausewitz received five Solution-B night-fighting Panthers, and these vehicles entered combat for their first and last time near Uelzen. Before being overrun by the Allies, these vehicles managed to destroy several examples of the new British Comet tank. It is clear that these night-fighting experiments failed to justify the time and expense devoted to them.

PANTHER ARMOURED OBSERVATION VEHICLE

Another very rare variant of the standard Panther tank was the *Panzerbeobachtungspanther*. This was an armoured artillery observation variant of the Panther, which was designed to serve with the self-propelled artillery battalion fielded by each panzer division. These battalions deployed *Wespe* (Wasp) medium self-propelled guns (*panzerartillerie*), based on the Panzer II chassis, and *Hummel* (Bumblebee) heavy vehicles, based on the hybrid Panzer III/IV platform. The tactical role of the Observation Panther was to observe enemy targets – often while under enemy fire – and then calculate relevant ranges and bearings. The vehicle would then use its communications devices to convey

Below: The crew of a Jagdpanther take the opportunity to ride on the deck of the tank. The tough towing cables needed to tow the Jagdpanther out of trouble can be seen above the side skirts.

this targeting data to the Wespe and Hummel vehicles so that they could engage these enemy assets.

During 1944, the *Panzerbeobachtungspanther* was produced in tiny numbers, perhaps as few as 41 vehicles. Some one or two Observation Panthers were issued to favoured panzer divisions, usually elite Wehrmacht divisions like the *Grossdeutschland* or those of the Waffen-SS. In mid-December 1944, for example, the 12th SS Panzer Division *Hitlerjugend* fielded five *Panzerbeobachtungspanthers*, about 12 per cent of the total number built. Less-favoured armoured divisions probably never received a single vehicle.

The prototype *Panzerbeobachtungspanther* was completed during summer 1943, built on the chassis of a late-design Ausf D tank. The main production versions appeared from January 1944, with these initially being based upon the Panther Ausf A and then the Ausf G chassis. The *Panzerbeobachtungspanther* constituted a more potent battlefield asset because, unlike earlier armoured artillery observation vehicles based on the Panzer III, it retained its parent tank's main armament. In addition, these 41 Panther-based vehicles carried more sophisticated observation instruments, for the Panther vehicle commander had at his disposal two tall vision periscopes, instead of the single device featured in the *Artillerie-Panzerbeobachtungspanzer* (Sdkfz 143) and the *Panzerbeobachtungswagen* IV. In addition to its twin periscopes, the Observation Panther also mounted a powerful stereoscopic range-finder inside its turret.

The *Panzerbeobachtungspanther* was the most effective German armoured observation vehicle of World War II. The vehicle enjoyed the good level of armour protection which was standard in its parent Panther tank. It also retained the Panther tank's main armament, the potent 75mm L/70 gun, which further increased its battlefield survivability. Its advanced observation and communication devices enabled it to undertake more accurate artillery spotting. The only factor which undermined its impact on the battlefield was that

it was produced in such tiny numbers. which made it highly sought after by all panzer artillery battalion commanders.

JAGDPANTHER

In mid-1943 the German High Command tasked the MIAG firm to develop a prototype heavy tank destroyer based on the chassis of the Panther tank. The vehicle's specifications required that it mount the potent 88mm PaK 43/3 L/71 gun within a well-sloped armoured superstructure. By mid-October 1943, MIAG had produced a prototype Jagdpanther vehicle based on the Panther Ausf A. The Germans decided to proceed because they desperately needed an effective platform for the lethal 88mm L/71 gun. Previous improvised tank destroyers based on the hybrid Panzer III/IV chassis which carried the 88mm L/71 gun, such as the Nashorn (Rhinoceros), had proved unsatisfactory. This chassis could only support the gun if the vehicle's superstructure armour was left very thin to save weight; consequently, such vehicles could not withstand the increasing lethality of recent anti-tank rounds. Therefore construction of the Nashorn was ended in early 1944 in favour of the Jagdpanther.

The first production Jagdpanthers – based on the new Ausf G Panther chassis – rolled off the MIAG assembly lines in February 1944. This vehicle weighed a considerable 46.2 tonnes (45.5 tons), and featured moderately heavy armour some 80mm (3.2in) thick at the front and 50mm (2in) thick on the sides. However, the level of protection afforded by this armour was enhanced because these plates were set at deeply sloping angles (between 35 and 60 degrees) to maximise shot deflection. These well-sloped surfaces also contributed to the vehicle's low silhouette, which further increased its survivability on the battlefield. The vehicle's main armament, the 88mm PaK 43/3 L/71, could traverse just 11 degrees to the left and right. To engage targets at a greater angle the whole vehicle had to be moved, the enduring weakness of all limited-traverse tank destroyers. In addition,

the Jagdpanther also carried a ball-mounted 7.92mm MG 34 set in the hull front for close defence fire.

Despite being relatively heavy, the Jagdpanther was neither slow nor immobile. The vehicle, powered by the potent 12-cylinder Maybach HL230 700bhp engine, enjoyed good mobility thanks to its wide tracks and suspension. This combination gave the vehicle a modest ground pressure figure, lower even than the much lighter and smaller StuG III assault gun. As a result, the tank destroyer could deliver both road and cross-country performances to put most of its rival vehicles in the shade. In fact, the Jagdpanther could obtain a maximum road speed of 45k/h (28m/h) and a still-respectable top cross-country speed of 24k/h (15m/h).

The Jagdpanther was Germany's most effective tank destroyer of the war, combining an effective trade-off between lethal firepower, good protection, and excellent mobility. The Germans manufactured the Jagdpanther from February 1944 until April 1945, when German tank production collapsed in the face of the Allied advance. During this period, the German Army received just 382 completed vehicles, making for a modest average production rate of 26 vehicles per month. During the first 10 months of the production run, MIAG was the sole manufacturer of Jagdpanthers, but from December 1944, MNH joined production in an attempt to boost delivery rates to 150 vehicles per month. That Jagdpanther deliveries never came close to these targets owed much to Allied bombing, and the consequent bottlenecks in certain key sub-components. Whatever the cause, the Germans simply never could field sufficient numbers of the Jagdpanther on the 1944–45 battlefield. If they had, then the Allies would have experienced greater difficulty completing their destruction of the Nazi Reich.

Below: Another view of the Jagdpanther. It carried the fearsome 88mm (3.46in) L/71 gun, also mounted in the King Tiger, which was more than capable of destroying any Allied tank.

Panzerkampfwagen V Panther Ausf G Specifications

Crew	5
Hull Length	6.88m (22.5ft)
Length Gun Forward	8.86m (29ft)
Width	3.43m (11.25ft)
Height	3.10m (10.1ft)
Combat Weight	44.8 tonnes (44 tons)
Ground Pressure	0.88kg (1.94lb)/cm^2

Ground Clearance	0.56m (1.8ft)
Fording Depth, without preparation	1.7m (5.5ft)
Fording Depth, with preparation	4m (13ft) - full water proofing never fully developed and not 100 per cent effective on production vehicles
Maximum Gradient	35 degrees
Maximum Trench Crossing	1.91m (6.2ft)
Maximum Step Climb	0.91m (2.9ft)

Suspension Type	lateral transverse torsion bars
No. of Road Wheel Sets	8 per side
Road Wheel Sets per Torsion Bar	1
Road Wheels per Set	2
Return Rollers	0
Wheel Size	800mm (3.14in) diameter
Tyres	rubber and later composite rubber/steel

Power Plant	Maybach HL 230 P30 petrol
Configuration	V-12 @ 60 degrees vec
Nominal Output	700 @ 3000 rpm
Nominal Efficiency	30.4 hp/litre
Power/Weight Ratio	15.6 hp/tonne
Capacity	2886 cc
Bore	130mm (5.1in)
Stroke	145mm (5.7in)
Compression Ratio	6.8:1
Aspiration	4 x solex 52 FFJ

Crank Shaft Bearings Lubrication System	dry sump
Oil Capacity	25 litres (5.4 gallons)
Coolant Type	water
Fuel Capacity	730 litres (160.5 gallons)
Road Range	177km (110 miles)
Cross Country Range	89km (55.3 miles)

Maximum Speed	46km/h (28.5 miles) - after November 1943 when HL 230 P30 regulated to not exceed 2500 rpm
Average Sustained Road Speed	30–35km/h (18.6–21.7 miles)
Average Cross Country Speed	20 km/h (12.4 miles)
Transmission	all-claw AK 7-200, 7 fwd 1R
Final Drive	epicyclic
Driven Sprocket	front
Steering Type	discontinuous regenerative type, providing 1 radius of turn for each gear engaged
Maximum Turn Radius	79m (259ft)
Minimum Turn Radius	10m (33ft)

Main Armament	75mm (2.9in) KwK 42 L/70 rifled cannon
Secondary Armament	2 7.92 MG 34 M-Gs, 1 coaxial, 1 hull mounted
Auxiliary Armament	1 7.92 MG 34 AA M-G optional Smoke7/N5N, 19mm (0.75in) Machine Pistol, 9mm (0.35in) pistols
Main Armament Ammunition	82
Secondary Armament Ammunition	4200

Armour	
Hull Front	80mm (3.15in) @ 55 degrees
Hull Side Upper	50mm (1.96in) @ 60 degrees
Hull Side Lower	40mm (1.57in) @ 90 degrees
Hull Rear	40mm (1.57in) @ 30 degrees
Hull Top	40–16mm (1.57–0.6in) @ 90 degrees
Hull Bottom	25–16mm (0.9–0.6in) @ 90 degrees
Turret Front	100mm (3.9in) @ 12 degrees
Sides	45mm (1.7in) @ 25 degrees
Mantel	100mm (3.9in) curved
Rear	45mm (1.7in) @ 25 degrees
Top	16 mm (0.6in) @ 90 degrees
Turret Traverse	hydraulic manual, after November 1943 360 degrees in 18 seconds
Traverse Rate	36 degrees in 15 seconds
Elevation Method	hand
Elevation Range	+20 to -4
Stabilisation	none

Variant Specifications

JAGDPANZER V JAGDPANTHER (SDKFZ 173)

Crew	5
Weight	45.5 tonnes (44.8 tons)
Overall Length	9.86m (32ft 4in)
Hull Length	6.87m (22ft 6in)
Width	3.29m (10ft 9in)
Height	2.72m (8ft 11in)
Engine	Maybach HL230 P30 V12 cyclinder petrol
Power	700 bhp
Fuel Capacity	700 litres (154 gallons)
Speed	46km/h (29 miles)
Range	210km (131 miles) (road), 140km (87 miles) (cross-country)
Main Armament	8.8cm (3.5in) PaK 43/3 L/71 gun
Secondary Armament	one 7.92mm (0.312in) MG 34 machine gun
Armour	
Hull Front	60mm (2.4in) @ 35 degrees
Hull Side	40mm (1.6in) @ 90 degrees
Hull Rear	40mm (1.6in) @ 60 degrees
Hull Top	17mm (0.61in) @ 5 degrees
Superstructure Front	80mm (3.2in) @ 35 degrees
Superstructure Sides	50mm (2in) @ 60 degrees
Superstructure Rear	40mm (1.6in) @ 60 degress
Superstructure Roof	17mm (0.67in) @ 5 degrees

BERGEPANTHER (SD KFZ 179) ARMOURED RECOVERY VEHICLE

Crew	4
Weight	43.3 tonnes (42.7 tons)
Length	8.08m (26.5ft)
Height	2.74m (8.9ft)
Engine	Maybach HL230 P30
Gearbox	AK 7-400 7 forward 1 reverse
Speed	46km/h (28.5 miles)
Range	310km (192.6 miles) (road) 150km (93.2 miles) (cross-country)
Radio	FuG5
Main Armament	2cm (0.78in) KwK 38
Secondary Armament	one 7.92mm (0.31in) MG 34 machine gun
Armour	Rolled homogenous nickel steel plate
Hull Front	80mm (3.15in) @ 55 degrees
Hull Side	40mm (1.57in) vertical
Hull Rear	40mm (1.57in) @ 30 degrees
Hull Top	15mm (0.59in)

PANZERBEOBACHTUNGSWAGEN PANTHER ARTILLERY OBSERVATION VEHICLE

Crew	4
Weight	41.6 tonnes (41 tons)
Width	3.43m (11.25ft)
Length	6.88m (22.5ft)
Height	2.95m (9.6ft)
Engine	Maybach HL230 P30
Gearbox	AK 7-400 7 forward 1 reverse
Speed	46km/h (28.5 miles)
Range	210km (130.5 miles) (road) 100km (62.1 miles) (cross country)
Radio	FuG 8, FuG 4 and Funksprechgerät f
Armament	one 7.92mm (0.3in) MG 34 machine gun in turret, One 7.92mm (0.3in) MG 34 machine gun in hull
Armour	rolled homogenous nickle steel plate
Turret Front	100mm (3.9in)
Hull Front	80mm (3.1in)@ 55 degrees
Hull Side	40mm (1.57in) vertical
Hull Rear	40mm (1.57in) @ 30 degrees
Hull Top	15mm (0.59in)

The Panther's Main Rivals

VEHICLE	SHERMAN M4	T34 – 76A	CROMWELL MKV
Crew	Five	Four	Five
Hull length	5.85m (19.2ft)	6.1m (20ft)	6.24m (20.47ft)
Length, gun forward	5.85m (19.2ft)	6.1m (20ft)	6.4m (21ft)
Width	2.62m (8.6ft)	3.0m (9.84ft)	3.05m (10ft)
Height (to hatch)	2.74m (8.98ft)	2.45m (8ft)	2.46m (8ft)
Weight	30.25 tonnes (29.77 tons)	26.5 tonnes (26 tons)	27.9 tonnes (27.45 tons)
Ground pressure (kg sq cm)	1.1	0.64	0.95
Fording capacity	1.0m (3.28ft)	1.1m (3.6ft)	0.9/1.22m (2.95/4ft)
Gradient	60 per cent	70 per cent	47 per cent
Trench	2.3m (7.54ft)	3.0m (9.84ft)	2.3m (7.54ft)
Step	0.6m (1.96ft)	0.9m (2.95ft)	0.9m (2.95ft)
Suspension type	Vehicle voplute springs	Christie/coil springs	Christie/coil springs
Powerplant	R-975-C1 radial petrol	V-2-34 V-12 diesel	R-R Meteor V-12 petrol
Output	400hp	500hp	600hp
Power/weight ratio	13.22hp/tonne	19hp/tonne	21.5hp/tonne
Capacity	15,900cc	38,900cc	26,900cc
Fuel capacity	660 litres (174 gallons US)	420 litres (111 gallons US)	525 litres (138 gallons US)
Range, road	160km (100 miles)	450km (281 miles)	280km (175 miles)
Range, cross-country	–	260km (162.5 miles)	–
Nominal maximum speed	35kmph (21.9mph)	47kmph (29.37mph)	62kmph (38.75mph)
Steering type	Cletrac	Clutches	Regenerative
Turning radius	9.5m (31.16ft)	3.8m (12.46ft)	In place
Main armament	75mm (2.95in) L/40 M3	76.2mm (3in) L/30.5 M1938	75mm (2.95in) L36.5 Mk V
Secondary armament	Two 7.62mm (0.3in) M1919 MG	Two 7.62mm (0.3in) DT MG	Two 7.92mm (0.31in) Besa
Main armament ammunition	97 rounds	80 rounds	64 rounds (composite)
Secondary ammunition	4750 rounds	2400 rounds	4952 rounds
Armour	Cast/rolled, welded	Rolled, welded	Rolled, welded/riveted
Hull front	50.8mm (2in)	45mm (1.77in)	63mm (2.68in)
Hull sides	50.8mm (2in)	45mm (1.77in)	32mm (1.26in)
Hull rear	50.8mm (2in)	40mm (1.57in)	32mm (1.26in)
Hull top	19mm (.75in)	20mm (.78in)	20mm (.78in)
Hull bottom	19mm (.75in)	15mm (.59in)	14mm (.55in)
Turret front	76.2mm (3in)	45mm (1.77in)	76mm (2.3in)
Mantlet	90mm (3.54in)	–	–
Turret sides	76.2mm (3in)	45mm (1.77in)	63mm (2.48in)
Turret rear	76.2mm (3in)	40mm (1.57in)	57mm (2.24in)
Turret top	25.4mm (1in)	15mm (.59in)	20mm (.78in)
Turret traverse	Hydraulic/manual	Electric/manual	Hydraulic/manual
Elevation range (degrees)	+25 to -10 degrees	+30 to -3 degrees	+20 to -12.5 degrees
Stabilisation	Elevation	None	None

INDEX

95